TEACHING AGRICULTURAL
CONCEPTS

TEACHING AGRICULTURAL
C O N C E P T S

Farshad Ghooshchi

Assistant Professor in Department of Agronomy, Varamin-Pishva
Branch, Islamic Azad University, Varamin, Iran.

Lia Omidvar

Department of English Language and Translation, Varamin-Pishva
Branch, Islamic Azad University, Varamin, Iran.

authorHOUSE®

AuthorHouse™
1663 Liberty Drive
Bloomington, IN 47403
www.authorhouse.com
Phone: 1-800-839-8640

Published by AuthorHouse   04/16/2012

ISBN: 978-1-4685-7694-8 (sc)
ISBN: 978-1-4685-7693-1 (e)

Library of Congress Control Number: 2012906362

Contents

Chapter one
ECOLOGY

Ecology *[environmental science]* is usually considered as a branch of biology, the general science that studies living organisms. It is associated with the highest levels of biological organization, including the individual organism, the population, the ecological community, the ecosystem and the biosphere as a whole.

Because of its focus on the interrelations between organisms and their environment, ecology is a multidisciplinary science that draws on many other branches, including geology and geography, **meteorology** *[weather science]*, soil science, genetics, chemistry, physics, mathematics and statistics.

Ecology is also a highly applied science, especially with respect to issues of natural resource management. Efforts related to wildlife conservation, **habitat** *[residence]* management, **mitigation** *[reduction]* of ecological impacts of environmental pollution, ecosystem **restoration** *[revival]*, species reintroductions, fisheries, forestry and game management are often the direct domains of applied ecology. Urban development, agricultural and public health issues are also often informed by ecological perspectives and analysis.

Biosphere

For modern ecologists, ecology can be studied at several levels: population level (individuals of the same species in the same or similar environment), biocoenosis level (or community of species), ecosystem level, and biosphere level.

The outer layer of the planet Earth can be divided into several compartments: the hydrosphere (or sphere of water), the lithosphere (or sphere of soils and rocks), and the atmosphere (or sphere of the air). The biosphere (or sphere of life), sometimes described as "the fourth **envelope [*covering layer*]**," is all living matter on the planet or that portion of the planet occupied by life. It reaches well into the other three spheres, although there are no permanent inhabitants of the atmosphere. Relative to the volume of the Earth, the biosphere is only the very thin surface layer that extends from 11,000 meters below sea level to 15,000 meters above.

Ecosystem

A central principle of ecology is that each living organism has an ongoing and continual relationship with every other element that makes up its environment. The sum total of interacting living organisms (the biocoenosis) and their non-living environment (the biotope) in an area is termed an *ecosystem*. Studies of ecosystems usually focus on the movement of energy and matter through the system.

Almost all ecosystems run on energy captured from the sun by primary producers via photosynthesis. This energy then flows through the food chains to primary consumers (herbivores who eat and digest the plants), and on to secondary and tertiary consumers (either **carnivores [*meat-eater]*** or **omnivores [*eating all kinds of foods]***). Energy is lost to living organisms when it is used by the organisms to do work, or is lost as waste heat.

Matter is incorporated into living organisms by the primary producers. Photosynthetic plants fix carbon from carbon dioxide and nitrogen from atmospheric nitrogen or nitrates present in the soil to produce amino acids. Much of the carbon and nitrogen contained in ecosystems is created by such plants, and is then consumed by secondary and tertiary consumers and incorporated into them. Nutrients are usually returned to the ecosystem via **decomposition** *[breaking into parts]*. The entire movement of chemicals in an ecosystem is termed a biogeochemical cycle, and includes the carbon and nitrogen cycle.

Ecosystems of any size can be studied; for example, a rock and the plant life growing on it might be considered an ecosystem. This rock might be within a plain, with many such rocks, small grass, and grazing animals—also an ecosystem. This plain might be in the tundra, which is also an ecosystem (although once they are of this size, they are generally termed ecozones or **biomes** *[any major regional biological community]*). In fact, the entire terrestrial surface of the earth, all the matter which composes it, the air that is directly above it, and all the living organisms living within it can be considered as one, large ecosystem.

Biome

A biome is a homogeneous ecological formation that exists over a large region, such as tundra or steppes. The biosphere comprises all of the Earth's biomes—the entirety of places where life is possible—from the highest mountains to the depths of the oceans.

Biomes correspond rather well to subdivisions distributed along the **latitudes** *[the angular distance north or south from the equator]*, from the **equator** *[the great circle of the earth that is equidistant from the North Pole and South Pole]* towards the **poles** *[each of the extremities of the axis of the earth]*, with differences based on the physical environment (for example, oceans or mountain ranges) and the climate. Their variation is generally related to the distribution of species according to their ability to tolerate temperature, dryness, or both.

Though this is a simplification of a more complicated scheme, latitude and **altitude** *[the height of anything above a given reference]* approximate a good representation of the distribution of **biodiversity** *[diversity among and within plant and animal species]* within the biosphere. Very generally, the richness of biodiversity (as well for animal as for plant species) is decreasing most rapidly near the equator and less rapidly as one approach the poles.

The biosphere may also be divided into ecozones, which are very well defined today and primarily follow the continental borders. The ecozones are themselves divided into ecoregions, though there is not agreement on their limits.

a) Comprehension Questions

1. What branch of science does ecology belong to?
2. Name direct domains of applied ecology?
3. In what levels can ecology be studied?
4. What are biotope and biocoenosis?
5. Explain the main principal of ecology?
6. Where do the ecosystems mostly gain their energy?
7. How does photosynthesis happen?
8. Is there any limitation to the size of ecosystems to be studied? (Give an example)
9. What is biome?
10. What is equator?
11. Where can biodiversity be seen less than other places?
12. What are ecozones and ecoregions?

b) Good to know!

Generally, an ecological crisis occurs with the loss of adaptive capacity when the resilience of an environment or of a species or a population evolves in a way unfavorable to coping with perturbations that interfere with that ecosystem, landscape or species survival. It may be that the environment quality degrades compared to the species needs, after a change in an abiotic ecological factor (for example, an increase of temperature, less significant rainfalls). It may be that the environment becomes unfavorable for the survival of a species (or a population) due to an increased pressure of predation (for example overfishing). Lastly, it may be that the situation becomes unfavorable to the quality of life of the species (or the population) due to a rise in the number of individuals (overpopulation).

According to its degree of endemism, a local crisis will have more or less significant consequences, from the death of many individuals to the total extinction of a species. Whatever its origin, disappearance of one or several species often will involve a rupture in the food chain, further impacting the survival of other species.

c) Internet Activity—Biological Control

Go to this website *http://www.science.org.au/nova/001/001key.htm* **and then answer these questions.**

1. Define Biological Control. _____

   _____

2. Why is biological control used mainly against introduced species?

3. State 2 successful examples of biological control.

4. Why must biological control agents be thoroughly tested before release? Justify your response.

5. Complete the events on the timeline of the calicivirus:

   1984_____

   1991_____

   1995_____

   Oct 1995_____

   April 1996_____

   August 1996_____

   Sept/Oct 1996_____

6. Go to Activities and complete Activity 1. Draw the graph on the back of this sheet. Complete questions (a) to (f) in the spaces below.

   (a)_____

   _____

   (b)_____

   _____

(c)_____

_____

(d)_____

_____

(e)_____

_____

(f)_____

_____

d) **Please visit Site: http://mbgnet.mobot.org/-Missouri Botanical Gardens and browse each biome then fill out the chart below. A few examples for plants/animals are fine.**

Biome	Type of Plants	Types of Animals	Details & Climate (weather)
Rainforest			
Tundra			
Taiga			
Desert			
Temperate (deciduous forest)			
Grasslands			

Browse the site to find the answers

1. Describe the leaves of trees that live in the taiga.
2. How do trees in the taiga protect themselves from fire?
3. The changing of seasons is best viewed in which biome?
4. Second to the rainforest, which biome gets the most amount of rain?
5. Identify the leaves below. (HINT: You will need to find the leaf ID section)

6. What is the main difference between a hot and a cold desert (besides temperature)?
7. Name the four major deserts of North America.
8. What is the world's largest desert?
9. In order to be classified as a "tropical rain forest" a forest must be located between what two Tropics?
10. Where can you find a rain forest in the United States?
11. What is the difference between arctic tundra and alpine tundra?
12. Relative to rainfall, the tundra is most like what other biome?
13. What are the three types of grasslands found in the United States?
14. What are the two largest lakes in North America?
15. What are the main groups of algae found in freshwater lakes?
16. What kinds of plants make up the "forests" of temperate oceans?
17. What is the longest river in the world?
18. What kinds of animals live in tide pools (see the shoreline biome link)
19. List two threats to coral reefs.

Extra reading

e) Read this text about different Ecology Disciplines

Disciplines

Ecology is a broad discipline comprising many sub-disciplines. A common, broad classification, moving from lowest to highest complexity, where complexity is defined as the number of entities and processes in the system under study, is:

- Ecophysiology examines how the physiological functions of organisms influence the way they interact with the environment, both biotic and abiotic.
- Population ecology studies the dynamics of populations of a single species.
- Community ecology (or **synecology**) focuses on the interactions between species within an ecological community.
- Ecosystem ecology studies the flows of energy and matter through the biotic and abiotic components of ecosystems.
- Landscape ecology examines processes and relationship in a spatially explicit manner, often across multiple ecosystems or very large geographic areas.
- Evolutionary ecology studies ecology in a way that explicitly considers the evolutionary histories of species and their interactions.
- Political ecology connects politics and economy to problems of environmental control and ecological change.

LET'S HAVE SOME FUN!

f)   PICTIONARY GAME—ECOLOGY

RULES

- ✏ PLAYERS MUST WORK IN PAIRS. (2 OR 3 PAIRS PER GAME)

- ✏ WITHIN THE PAIRS THE PLAYERS TAKE TURNS IN DRAWING AND GUESSING THE WORDS.

- ✏ ONE OF THE MEMBERS OF THE PAIR PICKS UP A CARD FROM THE DECK AND MUST NOT SHOW THEIR PARTNER

- ✏ ONCE THIS CARD HAS BEEN SEEN BY THIS PERSON, THE CARD THEN GOES TO THE PERSON IN THE OTHER PAIR THAT IS DRAWING—ONLY THE PEOPLE DRAWING CAN SEE THE CARD

- ✏ ONCE THE CARD HAS BEEN SEEN BY ALL PEOPLE THAT ARE DRAWING THE TIMER IS STARTED AND DRAWING BEGINS.
- ✏ THE OTHER MEMBER OF THE PAIR MUST THEN TRY TO GUESS WHAT THEIR PARTNER IS DRAWING—REMEMBER IT IS RELATED TO YOUR BIOLOGY WORK . . . .

- ✏ THE FIRST PAIR TO GUESS THE CORRECT ANSWER IS THE WINNER

- ✏ TO CALCULATE THE POINTS FOR YOUR PAIR ADD ONE POINT TO YOUR SCORE EVERY TIME YOU ARE THE FIRST TO WIN.

- ✏ WINNERS MAY RECEIVE PRIZES SO MAKE AN EFFORT!!!!

CARDS TO CUT UP

ENVIRONMENT	FOOD CHAIN	FOOD WEB
HERBIVORE	CARNIVORE	OMNIVORE
PRODUCER	SCAVENGER	PREDATOR
PREY	PARASITE	DECOMPOSER
BIOLOGICAL CONTROL	BIOLOGICAL MAGNIFICATION	DETRITUS
HABITAT	CARBON DIOXIDE	OXYGEN
RESPIRATION	PHOTOSYNTHESIS	SUNLIGHT

g) Biome Web quest

Check these websites as a resource to biome. You will find them helpful.

Resources

Biomes of the World

http://www.snowcrest.net/
geography/slides/biomes/index.html

Learn about Biomes

http://www.richmond.edu/~ed344/
webunits/biomes/biomes.html

Nearctica Biomes

http://www.nearctica.com/educate/
subject/biomes.htm

Biomes and Habitats

http://www.enchantedlearning.
com/biomes/

The World's Biomes

http://www.ucmp.berkeley.edu/glossary/
gloss5/biome/

Tropical Rainforests and Other Biomes

http://www.panda.org/kids/wildlife/
mntropic.htm

Biomes of the World

http://www.teachersfirst.com/lessons/
biomes/biomes.html

Introduction to Biomes

http://www.runet.edu/~swoodwar/
CLASSES/GEOG235/biomes/intro.html

Chapter two
Crops I

1) Cereals

Cereals, grains or cereal grains, are grasses cultivated for the edible components of their fruit seeds—the **endocarp** *[the hard inner layer of the pericarp of some fruits]*, **germ** *[The small mass of cells from which a new organism develops]* and **bran** *[hard outer layer of grain]*. Cereal grains are grown in greater quantities and provide more food energy worldwide than any other type of crop; they are therefore **staple crops** *[crop that can be stored for use throughout the year]*. In their natural form (as in whole grain), they are a rich source of vitamins, minerals, carbohydrates, fats and oils, and protein. However, when refined by the removal of the bran and germ, the remaining endocarp is mostly carbohydrate and lacks the majority of the other nutrients. In some developing nations, grain in the form of rice, wheat, or maize (in American terminology, corn) constitutes a majority of daily sustenance.

Farming

While each individual species has its own features, the cultivation of all cereal crops is similar. All are annual plants; consequently one planting yields one harvest. Wheat, **rye *[edible grain]***, triticale, oats, barley, and spelt are the cool-season cereals. These are **hardy plants *[plants resistant to pests and diseases]*** that grow well in moderate weather and cease to grow in hot weather (approximately 30°C but this varies by species and variety). The other warm-season cereals are tender and prefer hot weather.

Barley and rye are the hardiest cereals, able to overwinter in the subarctic and Siberia. Many cool-season cereals are grown in the tropics. However, some are only grown in cooler highlands, where it may be possible to grow multiple crops in a year.

Planting

The warm-season cereals are grown in tropical lowlands year-round and in **temperate *[moderate]*** climates during the frost-free season. Rice is commonly grown in flooded fields, though some strains are grown on dry land. Other warm climate cereals, such as sorghum, are adapted to **arid *[extremely dry]*** conditions.

Cool-season cereals are well-adapted to temperate climates. Most varieties of a particular species are either winter or spring types. Winter varieties are **sown *[sprinkled with seed]*** in the autumn, germinate and grow vegetatively, then become dormant during winter. They resume growing in the springtime and **mature *[grown]*** in late spring or early summer. This cultivation system makes optimal use of water and frees the land for another crop early in the growing season. Winter varieties do not flower until springtime because they require vernalization: exposure to low temperature for a genetically determined length of time. Where winters are too warm for vernalization or exceed the hardiness of the crop (which varies by species and variety), farmers grow spring varieties. Spring cereals are planted in early springtime and mature later that same summer, without vernalization. Spring cereals typically require more irrigation and yield less than winter cereals.

Grow season

Once the cereal plants have grown their seeds, they have completed their life cycle. The plants die and become brown and dry. As soon as the parent plants and their seed **kernels** *[the inner part of a seed]* are reasonably dry, harvest can begin.

In developed countries, cereal crops are universally machine-harvested, typically using a combine harvester, which cuts, threshes, and winnows the grain during a single pass across the field. In developing countries, a variety of harvesting methods are in use, from combines to hand tools such as the scythe or cradle.

Rice

Rice is the seed of the monocot plant of the grass family (Poaceae). As a cereal grain, it is the most important staple food for a large part of the world's human population, especially in tropical Latin America, the West Indies, East, South and Southeast Asia. It is the grain with the second highest worldwide production, after maize ("corn"). Since a large portion of maize crops are grown for purposes other than human consumption, rice is probably the most important grain with regards to human nutrition and caloric **intake** *[consumption]*, providing more than one fifth of the calories consumed worldwide by the human species.

Rice is normally grown as an annual plant, although in tropical areas it can survive as a perennial and can produce a ratoon crop for up to 20 years. The rice plant can grow to 1-1.8 m tall, occasionally more depending on the variety and soil **fertility[readiness to produce]**. The grass has long, **slender [thin]** leaves 50-100 cm long and 2-2.5 cm broad. The small wind-pollinated flowers are produced in a branched arching to **pendulous [hanging]** inflorescence 30-50 cm long. The edible seed is a grain (caryopsis) 5-12 mm long and 2-3 mm thick.

Rice can be grown practically anywhere, even on a steep hill or mountain. Although its parent species are native to South Asia and certain parts of Africa, centuries of trade and exportation have made it commonplace in many cultures worldwide.

The traditional method for cultivating rice is flooding the fields whilst, or after, setting the young **seedlings [young plant grown from seed]**. This simple method requires sound planning and servicing of the **water damming [to provide water with a dam]** and channeling, but reduces the growth of less robust weed and pest plants that have no submerged growth state, and **deters [prevent]** vermin. While with rice growing and cultivation the flooding is not mandatory, all other methods of irrigation require higher effort in weed and pest control during growth periods and a different approach for fertilizing the soil.

Wheat

Wheat is a worldwide cultivated grass from the Fertile Crescent region of the Near East. Wheat grain is a staple food used to make flour for leavened, flat and steamed breads; cookies, cakes, breakfast cereal, pasta, juice, noodles and couscous. Wheat is planted to a limited extent as a forage crop for livestock, and the straw can be used as fodder for livestock or as a construction material for roofing thatch.

Agronomy

While winter wheat lies dormant during a winter freeze, wheat normally requires between 110 and 130 days between planting and harvest, depending upon climate, seed type, and soil conditions. Crop management decisions require the knowledge of stage of development of the crop. In particular, spring fertilizer applications, herbicides, fungicides, growth regulators are typically applied at specific stages of plant development.

For example, current recommendations often indicate the second application of nitrogen be done when the ear (not visible at this stage) is about 1 cm in size. Knowledge of stages is also interesting to identify periods of higher risk, in terms of climate. For example, the meiosis stage is extremely susceptible to low temperatures (under 4 °C) or high temperatures (over 25 °C). Farmers also benefit from knowing when the flag leaf (last leaf) appears as this leaf represents about 75% of photosynthesis reactions during the grain-filling period and as such should be preserved from disease or insect attacks to ensure a good yield.

- *Wheat at the anthesis stage*

Maize

Maize also known as Indian corn but generically and usually shortened to corn is a cereal grain domesticated in Mesoamerica and subsequently spread throughout the American continents.

Maize is the most widely grown crop in the Americas (332 million metric tons annually in the United States alone). Hybrid maize is preferred by farmers over conventional varieties. While some maize varieties grow up to 7 meters tall, most commercially grown maize has been bred for a standardized height of 2.5 meters. Sweet corn is usually shorter than field-corn varieties.

Seeds

The kernel of maize has a pericarp of the fruit **fused** *[blend]* with the seed coat, typical of the grasses. It is close to a multiple fruit in structure, except that the individual fruits (the kernels) never fuse into a single mass. The grains are about the size of peas, and adhere in regular rows round a white **pithy** *[compressed, short]* substance, which forms the ear. An ear contains from 200 to 400 kernels, and is from 10-25 centimeters in length. They are of various colors: blackish, bluish-gray, red, white and yellow. When ground into flour, maize yields more flour, with much less bran, than wheat does. However, it lacks the protein gluten of wheat and, therefore, makes baked goods with poor rising capability and coherence.

A genetic variation that accumulates more sugar and less starch in the ear is consumed as a vegetable and is called sweet corn.

Due to its shallow roots of only one to two inches deep, maize is susceptible to droughts, intolerant of nutrient-deficient soils, and prone to be uprooted by severe winds.

2) Fodder

In agriculture, **fodder** *[food, usually green leaves or seed pods, for livestock]* or animal feed is any foodstuff that is used specifically to feed domesticated livestock, such as cattle, goats, sheep, horses, chickens and pigs. Most animal feed is from plants but some is of animal origin. "Fodder" refers particularly to food given to the animals rather than that which they forage for themselves. It includes hay, straw, silage, compressed and pelleted feeds, oils and mixed rations, and also **sprouted** *[new growth of a plant]* grains and legumes.

Alfalfa

Alfalfa *[A plant, Medicago sativa, grown as a pasture crop]* is a flowering plant in the pea family Fabaceae cultivated as an important forage crop. In the UK, Australia and New Zealand it is known as lucerne and as lucerne grass in south Asia.

Alfalfa is a cool season perennial legume living from three to twelve years, depending on variety and climate. It resembles clover with clusters of small purple flowers. The plant grows to a height of up to 1 meter and has a deep root system sometimes stretching to 4.5 meters. This makes it very **resilient *[elastic]***, especially to droughts. It has a tetraploid genome. The plant exhibits autotoxicity, which means that it is difficult for alfalfa seed to grow in existing stands of alfalfa. Therefore, it is recommended that alfalfa fields be rotated with other species (for example, corn or wheat) before reseeding.

Like other legumes its root nodules contain bacteria with the ability to fix nitrogen, producing a high-protein feed regardless of available nitrogen in the soil. Its nitrogen-fixing abilities (which increase soil nitrogen) and its use as an animal feed greatly improved agricultural efficiency. (The nitrogen comes from the air, which is 78 percent molecular nitrogen.)

Alfalfa is widely grown throughout the world as forage for cattle, and is most often harvested as hay, but can also be made into silage, grazed, or fed as green chop. Alfalfa has the highest feeding value of all common hay crops, being used less frequently as pasture. When grown on soils where it is well-adapted, alfalfa is the highest yielding forage plant.

Alfalfa is one of the most important legumes used in agriculture. Its primary use is as feed for dairy cattle—because of its high protein content and highly digestible fiber—and secondarily for beef cattle, horses, sheep, and goats. Humans also eat alfalfa sprouts in salads and sandwiches. Tender shoots are eaten in some places as a leaf vegetable. Human consumption of fresh mature plant parts is rare and limited primarily by alfalfa's high fiber content. Dehydrated alfalfa leaf is commercially available as a dietary supplement in several forms, such as tablets, powders and tea.

Culture

Alfalfa can be sown in spring or fall, and does best on well-drained soils with a neutral pH of 6.8-7.5. Alfalfa requires a great deal of potassium to grow well. It is moderately sensitive to salt levels in both the soil and in irrigation water, although it continues to be grown in the arid southwest USA where salinity is an emerging issue. Soils low in fertility should be fertilized with manure or a chemical fertilizer, but correction of pH is particularly important. Usually a seeding rate of 13-20 kg/hectare is recommended, with differences based upon region, soil type, and seeding method. A **nurse crop** *[annual crop that provides rapid soil stabilization]* is sometimes used, particularly for spring plantings, to reduce weed problems. Herbicides are sometimes used in place of the nurse crop, particularly in Western production.

In most climates alfalfa is cut three to four times a year but is harvested up to 12 times per year in Arizona and southern California. Total yields are typically around 8 tons per hectare but yields have been recorded up to 20 t/ha. Yields vary with region, weather, and the crop's stage of maturity when cut. Later cuttings improve yield but reduce nutritional content.

Alfalfa is considered an 'insectary' due to the large number of insects it attracts. Some pests such as Alfalfa weevil, aphids, armyworms, and the potato leafhopper can reduce alfalfa yields dramatically, particularly with the second cutting when weather is warmest. Chemical controls are sometimes used to prevent this. Alfalfa is also susceptible to root rots including *Phytophthora*, *Rhizoctonia*, and Texas Root Rot.

a) Comprehension Questions

1. Name different kinds of cereals.
2. How is the cultivation of cereal crops?
3. How are cool-season and warm-season crops planted?
4. What are the main features of rice?
5. Explain the traditional method for cultivating rice.
6. In what conditions rice can be grown?
7. What does staple food mean?

8. What do crop management decisions require? Support your answer with an example.
9. What is maize and what are its characteristics?
10. What is a sweet corn?
11. Explain the characteristics of maize seeds.
12. Why maize is susceptible to droughts, intolerant of nutrient-deficient soils, and prone to be uprooted by severe winds?
13. What is Alfalfa and to what family does it belong?
14. What are the uses of Alfalfa?
15. In what condition can Alfalfa be grown?

b) Fill in the blanks with proper words

Resilience, staple crop, arid, seedling, fodder, kernel, slender, fused.

1. A region is said to be _____ when it is characterized by a severe lack of available water.
2. _____ is the inner and usually edible part of a seed or grain or nut or fruit stone.
3. The physical property of a material that can return to its original shape or position after deformation is called _____.
4. _____ means very narrow.
5. _____ means to become combined.
6. In agriculture, _____ is any foodstuff that is used specifically to feed domesticated livestock, such as cattle, goats, sheep, horses, chickens and pigs.
7. _____ is a food that can be stored for use throughout the year.

Good to know!
Major cultivated species of wheat

- **Common wheat** or **Bread wheat**—(*T. aestivum*) A hexaploid species that is the most widely cultivated in the world.
- **Durum**—(*T. durum*) The only tetraploid form of wheat widely used today, and the second most widely cultivated wheat.
- **Einkorn**—(*T. monococcum*) A diploid species with wild and cultivated variants. Domesticated at the same time as emmer wheat, but never reached the same importance.
- **Emmer**—(*T. dicoccon*) A tetraploid species, cultivated in ancient times but no longer in widespread use.
- **Spelt**—(*T. spelta*) another hexaploid species cultivated in limited quantities.

Nutrition

100 grams of hard red winter wheat contain about 12.6 grams of protein, 1.5 grams of total fat, 71 grams of carbohydrate, 12.2 grams of dietary fiber, and 3.2 mg of iron (17% of the daily requirement); the same weight of hard red spring wheat contains about 15.4 grams of protein, 1.9 grams of total fat, 68 grams of carbohydrate, 12.2 grams of dietary fiber, and 3.6 mg of iron (20% of the daily requirement).

Much of the carbohydrate fraction of wheat is starch. Wheat starch is an important commercial product of wheat, but second in economic value to wheat gluten. The principal parts of wheat flour are gluten and starch. These can be separated in a kind of home experiment, by mixing flour and water to form a small ball of dough, and kneading it gently while rinsing it in a bowl of water. The starch falls out of the dough and sinks to the bottom of the bowl, leaving behind a ball of gluten.

b) Extra reading

Alfalfa seed production requires the presence of pollinators when the fields of alfalfa are in bloom. Alfalfa pollination is somewhat problematic, however, because Western honey bees, the most commonly used pollinator, are not suitable for this purpose; the pollen-carrying keel of the Alfalfa flower trips and strikes pollinating bees on the head, which helps transfer the pollen to the foraging bee. Western honey bees, however, do not like being struck in the head repeatedly and learn to defeat this action by drawing nectar from the side of the flower. The bees thus collect the nectar but carry no pollen and so do not pollinate the next flower they visit. Because older, experienced bees don't pollinate alfalfa well, most pollination is accomplished by young bees that have not yet learned the trick of robbing the flower without tripping the head-knocking keel. When western honey bees are used to pollinate alfalfa, the beekeeper stocks the field at a very high rate to maximize the number of young bees.

c) Discuss the characteristics of the crops you have learnt in this lesson.

Chapter three
Crops II

Industrial crops

There are some groups of crops that are not used directly; rather there are some accumulations in some parts of the crop that must be extracted through some chemical and industrial processes in order to be used. These crops are divided into three major groups as: 1) oilseeds, like soybean, sunflower, canola, peanut, and sesame, 2) fiber plants, like cotton, kenaf, and flax, and 3) sugar plants, like sugar beet and cane.

1) Oilseeds

Soybean

The soybean (U.S.) or soya bean (UK) (*Glycine max*) is a species of legume native to East Asia. The plant is classed as an oilseed rather than a pulse. It is an annual plant that has been used in China for 5,000 years as a food and a component of drugs. Soy contains significant amounts of all the essential amino acids for humans, which makes soy a good protein source. Soybeans are the primary ingredient in many processed foods, including dairy product substitutes.

Soybeans are an important source of vegetable oil and protein worldwide. Soy products are the main ingredients in many meat and dairy substitutes. They are also used to make soy sauce, and the oil is used in many industrial applications. The main producers of soy are the United States, Brazil, Argentina, China and India. The beans contain significant amounts of alpha-linolenic acid, omega-6 fatty acid, and the isoflavones genistein and daidzein.

Description and physical characteristics

Soy varies in growth, habit, and height. It may grow **prostrate** *[horizontal]*, not higher than 20 cm (7.8 inches), or grow up to 2 meters (6.5 feet) high.

The **pods** *[the vessel that contains the seeds of a plant]*, stems, and leaves are covered with fine brown or gray hairs. The leaves are trifoliolate, having 3 to 4 **leaflets** *[part of a compound leaf]* per leaf, and the leaflets are 6-15 cm long and 2-7 cm broad. The leaves fall before the seeds are mature. The big, inconspicuous, self-fertile flowers are borne in the **axil** *[the angle between the upper side of a leaf and the supporting stem]* of the leaf and are white, pink or purple.

The fruit is a hairy pod that grows in clusters of 3-5; each pod is 3-8 cm long and usually contains 2-4 (rarely more) seeds 5-11 mm in diameter.

Soybeans occur in various sizes, and in many **hull** *[outer covering of a seed]* or seed coat colors, including black, brown, blue, yellow, green and mottled. The hull of the mature bean is hard, water resistant, and protects the cotyledon and hypocotyl (or "germ") from damage. If the seed coat is **cracked** *[broken]*, the seed will not germinate. The scar, visible on the seed coat, is called the hilum (colors include black, brown, buff, gray and yellow) and at one end of the hilum is the micropyle, or small opening in the seed coat which can allow the **absorption** *[uptake of substances by a tissue]* of water for sprouting.

Remarkably, seeds such as soybeans containing very high levels of protein can undergo **desiccation** *[dry up]* yet survive and revive after water absorption.

Cultivation

Cultivation is successful in climates with hot summers, with optimum growing conditions in mean temperatures of 20 °C to 30 °C; temperatures of below 20 °C and over 40 °C **retard** *[slow]* growth significantly. They can grow in a wide range of soils, with optimum growth in moist **alluvial** *[a deposit of sandformed by flowing water]* soils with a good organic content. Soybeans, like most legumes, perform nitrogen fixation by establishing a symbiotic relationship with the bacterium *Bradyrhizobium japonicum*. However, for best results an inoculum of the correct strain of bacteria should be mixed with the Soy bean (or any legume) seed before planting. Modern crop cultivars generally reach a height of around 1 m, and take 80-120 days from sowing to harvesting.

Sunflowers

Sunflowers are annual plants native to the Americas that possess a large inflorescence (flowering head). Sunflower stems can grow as high as 3m and the flower head can reach 30 cm in diameter with large edible seeds. The term "sunflower" is also used to refer to all plants of the genus *Helianthus*, many of which are perennial plants.

Description

Sunflower head displaying florets in spirals of 34 and 55 around the outside

What is usually called the flower is actually a *head* (formally *composite flower*) of numerous florets (small flowers) crowded together. The outer florets are the sterile *ray florets* and can be yellow, maroon, orange, or other colors. The florets inside the circular head are called *disc florets*, which mature into what are traditionally called "sunflower seeds," but are actually the fruit (an *achene*) of the plant. The inedible husk is the wall of the fruit and the true seed lies within the kernel.

The florets within the sunflower's cluster are arranged in a spiral pattern. Typically each floret is oriented toward the next by approximately the golden angle, 137.5°, producing a pattern of interconnecting spirals where the number of left spirals and the number of right spirals are successive **Fibonacci numbers** *[the unending sequence 1, 1, 2, 3, 5, . . . where each term is defined as the sum of its two predecessors.]*. Typically, there are 34 spirals in one direction and 55 in the other; on a very large sunflower there could be 89 in one direction and 144 in the other. This pattern produces the most efficient packing of seeds within the flower head.

Cultivation and uses

To grow well, sunflowers need full sun. They grow best in fertile, moist, well-drained soil with a lot of **mulch** *[protective covering of compost spread to reduce soil erosion]*. In commercial planting, seeds are planted 45 cm apart and 2.5 cm deep.

Sunflower "whole seed" (fruit) is sold as a snack food, after roasting in ovens, with or without salt added. Sunflowers can be processed into a peanut butter alternative, Sun butter.

Sunflower oil, extracted from the seeds, is used for cooking, as a carrier oil and to produce margarine and biodiesel, as it is cheaper than olive oil. A range of sunflower varieties exist with differing fatty acid compositions; some 'high oleic' types contain a higher level of healthy mono-unsaturated fats in their oil than even olive oil.

The **cake** *[a block of solid substance]* remaining after the seeds have been processed for oil is used as a livestock feed. Some recently developed cultivars have drooping heads. These cultivars are less attractive to gardeners growing the flowers as ornamental plants, but appeal to farmers, because they reduce bird damage and losses from some plant diseases. Sunflowers also produce **latex** *[a milky liquid in certain plants]* and are the subject of experiments to improve their suitability as an alternative crop for producing hypoallergenic rubber.

2) Fiber plants

Cotton

Cotton is a soft, staple fiber that grows in a form known as a **boll** *[a rounded seed vessel]* around the seeds of the cotton plant, a shrub native to tropical and subtropical regions around the world, including the Americas, India and Africa. The fiber most often is spun into yarn or thread and used to make a soft, breathable textile which is the most widely used natural-fiber cloth in clothing today.

Cultivation

Successful cultivation of cotton requires a long frost-free period, plenty of sunshine, and a moderate rainfall, usually from 600 to 1200 mm. Soils usually need to be fairly heavy, although the level of nutrients does not need to be exceptional. In general, these conditions are met within the seasonally dry tropics and subtropics in the Northern and Southern hemispheres, but a large proportion of the cotton grown today is cultivated in areas with less rainfall that obtain the water from irrigation. Production of the crop for a given year usually starts soon after harvesting the preceding autumn. Planting time in spring in the Northern hemisphere varies from the beginning of February to the beginning of June.

Pests and weeds

The cotton industry relies heavily on chemicals such as fertilizers and **insecticides** *[a substance for killing insects]*, although a very small number of farmers are moving toward an organic model of production and organic cotton products are now available for purchase at limited locations. These are popular for baby clothes and diapers. Under most definitions, organic products do not use genetic engineering.

Historically, in North America, one of the most economically destructive pests in cotton production has been the boll weevil. This pest has been eliminated from cotton in most of the United States. This program, along with the introduction of genetically engineered "Bt cotton" (which contains a bacteria gene that codes for a plant-produced protein that is toxic to a number of pests such as tobacco budworm, cotton bollworm, and pink bollworm), has allowed a reduction in the use of synthetic insecticides.

3) Sugar plants

Sugar beet

Sugar beet (*Beta vulgaris* L.), a member of the *Chenopodiaceae* family, is a plant whose root contains a high concentration of **sucrose** *[The sugar obtained from the sugar beet]*. It is grown commercially for sugar production.

The sugar beet is directly related to the beetroot, **chard** *[a variety of* *beet]* and fodder beet, all descended by cultivation from the sea beet.

The European Union, the United States, and Russia are the world's three largest sugar beet producers, although only the European Union and Ukraine are significant exporters of sugar from beets.

Culture

Sugar beet is a hardy biennial plant that can be grown commercially in a wide variety of temperate climates. During its first growing season, it produces a large (1-2 kg) storage root whose dry **mass** *[considerable* *portion]* is 15-20% sucrose by weight. If the plant is not harvested at this time, then during its second growing season, nutrients in the root will be used to produce flowers and seeds and the root will decrease in size. In commercial beet production, the root is harvested after the first growing season.

In most temperate climates, beets are planted in the spring and harvested in the autumn. At the northern end of its range growing seasons as short as 100 days can produce commercially viable sugar beet crops. In warmer climates sugar beets are a winter crop, planted in the autumn and harvested in the spring. In recent years, Syngenta AG has developed the so-called tropical sugar beet. It allows the plant to grow in tropical and subtropical regions. Beets are planted from a small seed; 1 kg of beet seed comprises 100,000 seeds and will plant over a hectare of ground.

a) Comprehension Questions

1. Name three main groups of industrial crops.
2. Is soy bean an oil seed or a pulse?
3. What are the nutrition information and usages of soybeans?
4. What are the physical characteristics of soybeans?
5. In what conditions can soybean be cultivated?
6. What is a floret and what are its features?
7. Describe the physical characteristics of sun flowers.
8. In what situations can sunflowers grow best?
9. What are sunflower products?

10. What is cotton and to what group of plants does it belong?
11. What soil features and weather conditions does cotton need in order to grow best?
12. Name a sugar plant and describe its needed condition to grow.
13. When can the sugar beets be harvested and planted?

b) Fill in the blanks with the proper words

Prostrate, crack, hull, absorb, sucrose, boll, mulch, latex, desiccation, retard.

1. _____ is the milky sap of several trees that coagulates on exposure to air; used to make rubber.
2. Most of the plants _____ carbon dioxide.
3. To _____ means to break something so that it does not separate, but very thin lines appear on its surface, or to become broken in this way.
4. _____ means stretched out and lying at full length along the ground horizontally.
5. Drying outer covering of a fruit or seed or nut is called _____.
6. _____ means slow the growth or development of something.
7. _____ is the protective covering of rotting vegetable matter spread to reduce evaporation and soil erosion.
8. _____ (common name: table sugar, also called saccharose) is a disaccharide of glucose and fructose.
9. The seed pod of the cotton plant is called _____.
10. _____ is the state of extreme dryness, or the process of extreme drying.

C) Extra Reading

Heliotropism

Sunflowers in the bud stage exhibit heliotropism. At sunrise, the faces of most sunflowers are turned towards the east. Over the course of the day, they follow the sun from east to west, while at night they return to an eastward orientation. This motion is performed by motor cells in the pulvinus, a flexible segment of the stem just below the bud. As the bud stage ends, the stem stiffens and the blooming stage is reached.

Sunflowers in their blooming stage lose their heliotropic capacity. The stem becomes "frozen", typically in an eastward orientation. The stem and leaves lose their green color.

The wild sunflower typically does not turn toward the sun; its flowering heads may face many directions when mature. However, the leaves typically exhibit some heliotropism.

d) Discussion

Please read this text about Genetically Modified Crops (GMC) carefully and discuss it in the class.

What is a genetically modified food product?

A tomato designed to stay fresh for a long time is one example of a genetically modified food. Corn designed to resist pesticides is another example.

Genetically modified food products are plants that have had their genetic characteristics altered. Scientists change the plants' characteristics by putting new genetic material into them, genes for example from bacteria which can withstand pesticides.

Advantages:

- The farmer can grow a larger crop because it is easier to fight pests.
- In some cases the farmer can use a more environmentally friendly crop spray.
- The farmer can also protect the environment by using less crop spray.

Disadvantages:

- Genes from the genetically modified rape crop could be transferred to the pests. The pests then become resistant to the crop spray and the crop spraying becomes useless.
- Rape plants can pollinate weeds.

Corn, soya beans and sugar cane have also been genetically modified by scientists so they are able to tolerate crop spray.

Insecticide sweet corn

Scientists have genetically modified sweet corn so that it produces a poison which kills harmful insects. This means the farmer no longer needs to fight insects with insecticides.

Advantages:

- The farmer no longer has to use insecticide to kill insects, so the surrounding environment is no longer exposed to large amounts of harmful insecticide.
- The farmer no longer needs to walk around with a drum of toxic spray wearing a mask and protective clothing.

Disadvantages:

- This type of genetically modified corn will poison the insects over a longer period than the farmer who would spray the crops once or twice. In this way the insects can become accustomed (or resistant) to the poison. If that happens both crop spraying and the use of genetically modified Bt-corn become ineffective.
- A variety of insects are at risk of being killed. It might be predatory insects that eat the harmful ones or, perhaps attractive insects such as butterflies. In the USA, where Bt-corn is used a great deal there is much debate over the harmful effects of Bt-corn on the beautiful Monarch butterfly.

Cotton and potatoes are other examples of plants that scientists have, genetically modified to produce insecticide.

examples of genetically modified crops

Pesticide resistant rape plants

Scientists have transferred a gene to the rape plant which enables the plant to resist a certain pesticide. When the farmer sprays his genetically modified rape crop with pesticides, he or she can destroy most of the pests without killing the rape plants.

e) **Write a paragraph on whether you are a pro or con of genetically modified crops and support your idea.**

Fun to Know

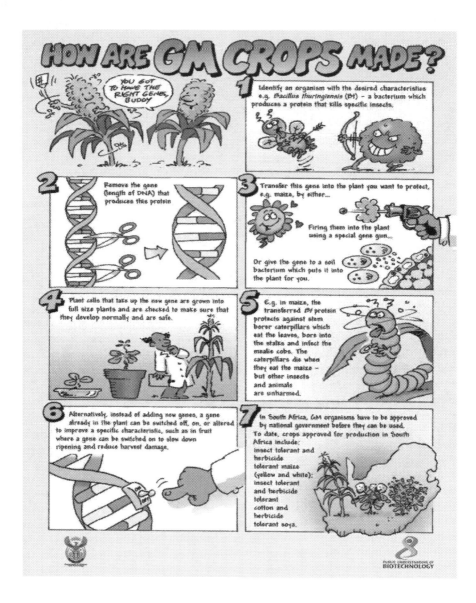

f) Good to know

Oil

In processing soybeans for oil extraction and subsequent soy flour production, selection of high quality, sound, clean, yellow soybeans are very important. Soybeans having a dark colored seed coat or even beans with a dark hilum will inadvertently leave dark specks in the flour, and are undesirable for use in commercial food products. All commercial soybeans in the United States are yellow or yellow brown.

To produce soybean oil, the soybeans are cracked, adjusted for moisture content, rolled into flakes and solvent-extracted with commercial hexane. The oil is then refined, blended for different applications, and sometimes hydrogenated. Soybean oils, both liquid and partially hydrogenated, are exported abroad, sold as "vegetable oil," or end up in a wide variety of processed foods. The remaining soybean husks are used mainly as animal feed.

Chapter four
Horticulture

Horticulture is the industry and science of plant cultivation. Horticulturists work and conduct research in the disciplines of **plant propagation** *[The process of reproducing or increasing plants]* and cultivation, crop production, **plant breeding** *[science of changing the genetics of plants for the benefit of humankind]* and genetic engineering, plant biochemistry, and plant physiology. The work particularly involves fruits, berries, nuts, vegetables, flowers, trees, **shrubs** *[A woody plant, a bush]*, and **turf** *[a layer of earth formed by grass]*. Horticulturists work to improve crop yield, quality, nutritional value, and **resistance** *[fighting]* to insects, diseases, and environmental stresses.

The study of horticulture

There is a thin border between the two terms, horticulture and gardening, although they are commonly used in a same meaning. Horticulture refers to the practice or science of growing flowers, fruit and vegetables, while gardening refers to the activity of working in a garden, growing plants, cutting lawn etc.

Gardening is the practice of growing ornamental or useful plants. Ornamental plants are normally grown for their flowers, foliage, or overall appearance. Useful plants may be grown for consumption (vegetables, fruits, herbs, or leaf vegetables) or for a variety of other purposes, such as medicines or **dyes** *[coloring agent]*.

Gardening ranges in scale from fruit orchards, to long boulevard plantings with one or more different types of shrubs, trees and herbaceous plants, to residential yards including lawns and foundation plantings, to large or small containers grown inside or outside. Gardening may be very specialized, with only one type of plant grown, or involve a large number of different plants in mixed plantings. It involves an active participation in the growing of plants, and tends to be **labor intensive** *[Requiring a great deal of work]*, which differentiates it from farming or forestry.

Organic horticulture

Organic horticulture is the science and art of growing fruits, vegetables, flowers, or ornamental plants by following the essential principles of organic agriculture in soil building and conservation, pest management, and **heirloom variety** *[a plant grown from seed over many generations]* preservation.

Horticulture is classically defined as the culture or growing of garden plants. Horticulture is also sometimes defined simply as "agriculture minus the plough." Instead of the plough, horticulture makes use of human labor and gardener's hand tools, although small machine tools like rotary tillers are common now.

Organic horticulture (or organic gardening) is based on knowledge and techniques gathered over thousands of years. In general terms, organic horticulture involves natural processes, often taking place over extended periods of time, and a sustainable, holistic approach—while chemical-based horticulture focuses on immediate, isolated effects and **reductionist** *[the analysis of complex things into simpler constituents]* strategies.

Fruit tree

A fruit tree is a tree bearing fruit that is consumed or used by people—all trees that are flowering plants produce fruit, which are the ripened **ovary** *[paired female reproductive organ that produces ova]* of a flower containing one or more seeds. In horticultural usage, the term 'fruit tree' is limited to those that provide fruit for human food. Types of fruits are described and defined elsewhere but would include fruit in a **culinary** *[able to be consumed]* sense as well as some nut bearing trees, like walnuts.

The scientific study and the cultivation of fruits is called pomology, which divides fruits into groups based on plant morphology and anatomy. Some of those groups are: **Pome** *[a fleshy fruit having seed chambers and an outer fleshy part]* fruits, which include apples and pears; and stone fruits which include peaches/nectarines, almonds, apricots, plums and cherries.

Examples of fruit trees

- Fruit tree propagation is usually carried out through asexual reproduction by grafting or budding the desired variety onto a suitable **rootstock** *[a root and its associated growth buds, used as a stock in plant propagation]*.

- Perennial plants can be propagated either by sexual or vegetative means. Sexual reproduction occurs when male **pollen** *[fertilizing element of flowering plants]* from one tree fertilizes the **ovules** *[female germ cell of a plant]* (**incipient** *[developing]* seeds) of the flower of another, stimulating the development of fruit. In turn this fruit contains a seed or seeds which, when **germinated** *[grow]*, will become a new **specimen** *[example]*. However, the new tree will inherit many of the characteristics of both its parents, and it will not grow 'true' to the variety from which it came. That is, it will be a fresh individual with many unpredictable characteristics of its own. Although this is desirable in terms of increasing biodiversity and the richness of the gene pool, only rarely will such fruit trees be directly useful or attractive to the tastes of humankind. A tendency to **revert** *[return to an earlier condition]* to a wild-like state is common.

- Therefore, from the **orchard** *[land for agriculture]* grower or gardener's point of view, it is preferable to propagate fruit cultivars vegetatively in order to ensure reliability. This involves taking a cutting (or **scion** *[a shoot one cut for planting]*) of wood from a desirable parent tree which is then grown on to produce a new plant or '**clone**' *[exact duplicate]* of the original.

Methods

The simplest method of propagating a tree asexually is rooting. A cutting (a piece of the parent plant) is cut and stuck into soil. Artificial rooting hormones are sometimes used to assure success. If the cutting does not die of **desiccation** *[dehydration]* first, roots grow from the buried portion of the cutting to become a complete plant. Though this works well for some plants (such as figs and olives), most fruit trees are unsuited to this method.

Root cuttings (pieces of root induced to grow a new **trunk** *[the main stem of a tree]*) are used with some kinds of plants. This method also is suitable only for some plants.

A refinement on rooting is layering. This is rooting a piece of a wood that is still attached to its parent and continues to receive nourishment from it.

The new plant is severed only after it has successfully grown roots. Layering is the technique most used for propagation of clonal apple rootstocks.

The most common method of propagating fruit trees, suitable for nearly all species, is grafting onto rootstocks. These are varieties selected for characteristics such as their **vigor *[energy]*** of growth, hardiness, soil **tolerance *[endurance]*,** and compatibility with the desired variety that will form the aerial part of the plant (called the scion). Two of the most common grafting techniques are 'whip and tongue', carried out in spring as the **sap *[the juice of a plant]*** rises, and 'budding', which is performed around July and August.

Vegetable

The term "vegetable" generally means the edible parts of plants. The definition of the word is traditional rather than scientific.

Mushrooms belong to the biological kingdom Fungi, not the plant kingdom, and yet they are also generally considered to be vegetables, at least in the **retail industry *[sale of goods]***. Nuts, seeds, grains, herbs, spices and culinary fruits are usually *not* considered to be vegetables, even though all of them are edible parts of plants. In general, vegetables are those plant parts that are regarded as being suitable to be part of **savory** ***[an aromatic plant of the mint family]*** or salted dishes, rather than sweet dishes. However, there are many exceptions, such as the pumpkin, which can be eaten as a vegetable in a savory dish, but which can also be sweetened and served in a pie as a dessert.

Some vegetables, such as carrots, bell peppers and celery, are eaten either raw or cooked; while others are eaten only when cooked.

a) Comprehension Questions

1. Define horticulture.
2. For what reasons is horticulture used?
3. In what sense horticulture and gardening are different?
4. In what areas can ornamental plants be seeded?
5. What is organic horticulture?
6. Which kinds of trees can produce fruits?
7. What is pomology and on what basis does it divide fruits?
8. What are fruit trees and what kind of fruit do they produce to be classified as fruit trees?
9. How fruit tree propagation is done?
10. How can perennial plants be propagated?
11. Describe sexual and vegetative production in perennial plants.
12. What are the methods for propagating a fruit tree?

b) Fill in the blanks with proper words.

Orchard, revert, plant breeding, ovule, culinary, dye, turf, shrub, trunk, clone

1. _____ means going back to a previous state.
2. _____ is a usually soluble substance for staining or coloring e.g. fabrics or hair.
3. The thick stem of a tree that the branches grow from is called_____
4. A _____ is a horticultural category of woody plant, distinguished from a tree by its multiple stems and lower height.
5. _____ is a piece of land where fruit trees are grown.

6. A small body that contains the female germ cell of a plant; develops into a seed after fertilization is called _____.

7. A_____ is a group of identical cells that share a common ancestry, meaning are derived from the same mother cell.

8. _____ is a layer of earth covered with grass; sod; a piece of such a layer cut from the soil and used to make a lawn.

9. _____ is the art and science of changing the genetics of plants for the benefit of humankind.

c) Good toKnow

Bud Grafting

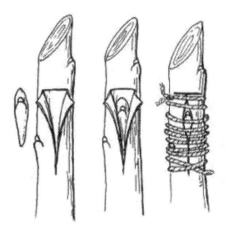

Diagram illustrating the bud grafting technique

1. Cut a slice of <u>bud</u> and <u>bark</u> from the <u>parent tree</u>.
2. Cut a similar sliver off the <u>rootstock</u>, making a little lip at the base to slot the scion into.
3. Join the two together and bind.
4. In time, the scion bud will grow into a <u>shoot</u>, which will develop into the desired <u>tree</u>.

Whip and tongue grafting

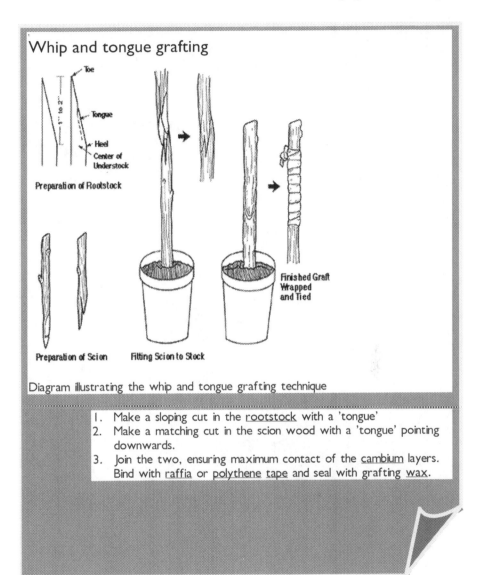

Preparation of Rootstock

Preparation of Scion   Fitting Scion to Stock

Finished Graft
Wrapped
and Tied

Diagram illustrating the whip and tongue grafting technique

1. Make a sloping cut in the <u>rootstock</u> with a 'tongue'
2. Make a matching cut in the scion wood with a 'tongue' pointing downwards.
3. Join the two, ensuring maximum contact of the <u>cambium</u> layers. Bind with <u>raffia</u> or <u>polythene tape</u> and seal with grafting <u>wax</u>.

d) Extra reading

Horticulture involves eight areas of study, which can be grouped into two broad sections—ornamentals and edibles:

- Arboriculture the study and selection, planting, care, and removal of individual trees, shrubs, vines, and other perennial woody plants.
- Floriculture includes production and marketing of floral crops.
- Landscape horticulture includes production, marketing and maintenance of landscape plants.
- Olericulture includes production and marketing of vegetables.
- Pomology includes production and marketing of fruits.
- Viticulture includes production and marketing of grapes.
- Postharvest physiology involves maintaining quality and preventing spoilage of horticultural crops.

Chapter five
Soil

Soil is the naturally occurring, unconsolidated or loose covering on the Earth's surface. Soil is composed of particles of broken rock that have been altered by chemical, biological and environmental processes including **weathering** *[to change because of weather conditions]* and **erosion** *[natural processes by which material is worn away from the earth's surface]*. Soil is different from its parent rock(s) source(s), altered by interactions between the **lithosphere** *[the solid portion of the earth]*, **hydrosphere** *[the water on the surface of the globe]*, **atmosphere** *[the mixture of gases that surrounds the earth]*, and the **biosphere** *[the ecosystem comprising the entire earth]*. It is a mixture of mineral and organic constituents that are in solid, gaseous and aqueous states. Soil particles pack loosely, forming a soil structure filled with pore spaces. These pores contain soil solution (liquid) and air (gas). Accordingly, soils are often treated as a three state system.

Soil forming factors

Soil formation, or pedogenesis, is the combined effect of physical, chemical, biological, and anthropogenic processes on soil parent material. Soil **genesis** *[creation]* involves processes that develop **layers** *[material spread over a surface]* or horizons in the soil profile. These processes involve additions, losses, transformations and translocations of material that compose the soil. Minerals derived from weathered rocks undergo changes that cause the formation of secondary minerals and other compounds that are variably soluble in water, these constitutes are moved from one area of the soil to other areas by water and animal activity. The alteration and movement of materials within soil causes the formation of distinctive soil horizons. The weathering of bedrock produces the parent material that soils form from. The plants are supported by the porous rock becoming filled with nutrient-bearing water, for example carrying dissolved bird droppings or guano. The developing plant roots, themselves or associated with **mycorrhizal *[fungus root]***, fungi gradually break up the porous lava, and organic matter soon accumulates. How the soil "life" cycle proceeds is influenced by at least five classic soil forming factors that are dynamically intertwined in shaping the way soil is developed, they include: parent material, regional climate, topography, biotic potential, and the passage of time.

Parent material

The material from which soils form is called parent material. It includes: weathered primary bedrock; secondary material transported from other locations. Few soils form directly from the breakdown of the underlying rocks they develop on. These soils are often called "residual soils", and have the same general chemistry as their parent rocks. Most soils derive from materials that have been transported from other locations by wind, water and gravity. The deeper sections of the soil profile may have materials that are relatively unchanged from when they were deposited by water, ice, or wind. Weather is the first stage in the transforming of parent material into soil material. The mineralogical and chemical composition of the primary bedrock material, plus physical features, including grain size and degree of **consolidation *[solidification]***, plus the rate and type of weathering, transforms it into different soil materials.

Climate

Soil formation greatly depends on the climate and soils from different climate zones show distinctive characteristics. Temperature and moisture affect weathering and **leaching *[percolating]***. Wind moves sand and other particles, especially in arid regions where there is little plant cover. The type and amount of **precipitation** *[moisture in air or falling from sky]* influence soil formation by affecting the movement of ions and particles through the soil, aiding in the development of different soil profiles. Temperature and precipitation rates affect biological activity, rates of chemical reactions, and types of vegetation cover.

Topography

Slope *[inclined surface]* and surface orientation affect the moisture and temperature of soil and the rate of weathering of parent material. Steep slopes facing the sun are warmer. Steep land may **erode** *[wear away]* faster than soil forms or material is **deposited** *[to lay by a natural process]*, causing a net loss of topsoil. Water in rivers and wind with strong enough currents deposit gravel, rocks, and sand, and remove smaller-sized particles which are deposited when the currents slow down.

Biological factors

Plants, animals, fungi, bacteria and humans affect soil formation. Animals and **micro-organisms** *[any organism too small to be viewed by eye]* mix soils and form **burrows** *[hole dug by animal]* and pores allowing moisture and gases to **seep** *[pass]* into deeper layers. In the same way, plant roots open channels in the soils, especially plants with deep **taproots** *[main root]* which can penetrate many meters through the different soil layers bringing up nutrients from deeper in the soil. Micro-organisms, including fungi and bacteria affect chemical exchanges between roots and soil and act as a reserve of nutrients. Humans can impact soil formation by removing vegetation cover, which promotes erosion.

Time

Time is a factor in the interactions of all the above factors as they develop soil. Over time, soils evolve features dependent on the other forming factors, and soil formation is a time-responsive process dependent on how the other factors interplay with each other. The long periods over which change occurs and its multiple influences mean that simple soils are rare, resulting in the formation of soil horizons.

Characteristics

Soil structure is the arrangement of soil particles into **aggregates [pile]**. These may have various shapes, sizes and degrees of development or expression. Soil structure affects **aeration [expose to air]**, water movement, resistance to erosion, and plant root growth. Structure often gives clues to texture, organic matter content, biological activity, past soil evolution and human use, and chemical and mineralogical conditions under which the soil formed.

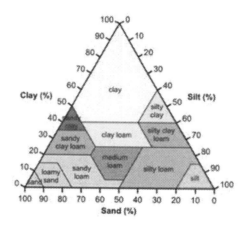

Soil texture refers to sand, **silt [fine sand]** and clay composition. Sand and silt are the product of physical weathering, while clay is the product of chemical weathering. Soil content affects soil behavior, including the retention capacity for nutrients and water. Clay soils resist wind and water erosion better than silty and sandy soils, because the particles are more tightly joined to each other. In medium textured soils, clay is often moved downward through the soil profile and accumulates in the **subsoil [the bed or of earth under the surface soil]**.

a) Comprehension questions

1. What is soil?
2. Explain weathering and erosion processes.
3. How is soil different from its parent rock?
4. What processes does soil genesis involve?
5. Name 5 factors that influence the soil life cycle.
6. What is the parent material and what does it include?
7. What is the first level in changing the parent material?
8. What are the factors that affect weathering and leaching?
9. How are burrows and pores made?
10. What is the characteristic of taproots?
11. What are micro-organisms?
12. Define soil structure.
13. What is soil texture?
14. What is the difference between sand and clay?

b) Fill in the blanks with proper words.

Burrow, slope, soil, erosion, biosphere, arid, weathering, deposite

1. The part of the earth's surface consisting of humus and disintegrated rock is called_____.
2. _____is the decomposition of earth rocks, soils and their minerals through direct contact with the planet's atmosphere.
3. Condition in which the earth's surface is worn away by the action of water and wind is called_____.
4. _____is the ground that has a natural incline, as the side of a hill.
5. A_____is a hole or tunnel dug into the ground by an animal to create a space suitable for habitation or temporary refuge.
6. All ecosystems on Earth as well as the Earth's crust, waters, and atmosphere on and in which organisms exist; also, the sum of all living matter on Earth is called_____.
7. A region is said to be_____when it is characterized by a severe lack of available water, to the extent of hindering the growth and development of plant and animal life.

c) Project

Based on your technical knowledge, write a paragraph about Soil forming factors.

d) Good to know!

Soil horizons

The naming of soil horizons is based on the type of material the horizons are composed of; these materials reflect the duration of the specific processes used in soil formation. They are labeled using a short hand notation of letters and numbers. They are described and classified by their color, size, texture, structure, consistency, root quantity, PH, and voids. Any one soil profile does not have all the major horizons covered below; soils may have few or many horizons.

The exposure of parent material to favorable conditions produces initial soils that are suitable for plant growth. Plant growth often results in the accumulation of organic residues; the accumulated organic layer is called the O horizon. Biological organisms colonize and break down organic materials, making available nutrients that other plants and animals can live on, and after sufficient time, a distinctive organic surface layer forms with humus which is called the A horizon.

e) Read the text below and answer the questions.

Soil Formation

Soil is a mixture of weathered rock and organic matter that usually covers bedrock (solid rock that underlies all soil). Both chemical and mechanical processes are involved in the development of soils.

- Chemical weathering turns hard minerals into soft ones
- Mechanical weathering breaks solid rock into smaller pieces
- Plant and animals add organic materials in the form of waste products and dead organisms

- The decay of organic matter produces acids which accelerate chemical weathering
- Burrowing Animals, such as earthworms, insects, and rodents, help circulate air and water through the soil and mix mineral and organic remains

The material from which soil forms is called its parent material. Soil that has weathered directly from the bedrock beneath it and therefore matches its parent material is called residual soil.

Soil that does not match the bedrock is called transported soil. It did not weather from the bedrock beneath it but was brought there by agents of erosion such as winds, rivers, or glaciers. Much of New England and the Midwest are covered by soil that was deposited by the movement of glaciers after the last Ice Age.

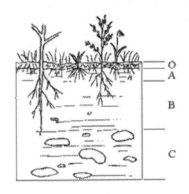

A cross section of soil exposed by digging is called the soil profile. The weathering of soil produces layers known as soil horizons. The topsoil or A horizon is usually rich in dark-colored organic remains called humus (labeled O horizon below). The subsoil or B horizon contains minerals that have been transported deeper by groundwater. Most of the clay in soil has also been washed down to this layer. The partially weathered bedrock or C horizon is composed of broken up bedrock on top of the solid bedrock (parent material).

Soil erosion is the removal of topsoil by the action of running water or wind. It takes between 100 and 400 years for one centimeter of topsoil to form.

Loss of topsoil can be caused when plants root are no longer present to hold down soil. Salting roads can raise the salinity of the soil and kill the plants. Over grazing can kill plants. Winds construction and mining can all effect plant cover.

Means of soil conservation include the following:

- Windbreaks—belts of trees along the edge of fields
- Contour farming—crops are planted in rows parallel to land contours
- Terraces—flattening hill slopes to slow the flow of water & erosion
- Strip Cropping—a crop that leaves bare ground between rows is alternated with a crop that completely covers the ground, ex. Corn & Alfalfa
- No-till method—plowing, planting and fertilizing are all done at the same time so there is less chance of wind removing topsoil

Use the worksheet above to answer the following questions.

1. Which layer in the diagram below contains the most organic material?
   A. A   B. B   C. C   D. the bedrock

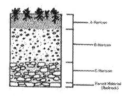

2. How is soil created from rock?
   A. physical weathering without chemical weathering
   B. chemical weathering without physical weathering
   C. erosion without weathering
   D. weathering without erosion

3. Approximately how many years does one centimeter of topsoil take to form?
   A. 100-400 years   C. 1000-4000 years

   B. 10-40 years   D. 10,000-40,000 years

4. Which of the following is found in the greatest % in soil?
   A. Mineral matter   B. Organic matter   C. Water   D. Air

5. Which layer of a soil profile forms first from the bedrock?

   A. A horizon   B. B horizon   C. C horizon   D. humus

6. For the soil profiles below, label the horizons (A, B, or C) and the parent material in each of the soil profiles using the spaces provided next to each image.

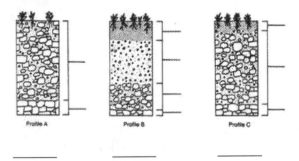

_____   _____   _____

7. At the base of each profile above, number the profiles according to the proper sequence of development.
8. Match each soil profile above to the graph below that would most likely represent that profile. Write the letter of the matching profile in the space provided below each graph.

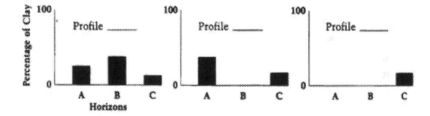

Chapter six
Fertilizer

Fertilizers *[plant food]* are chemical **compounds** *[mixture]* given to plants to promote **growth** *[development]*; they are usually applied either through the soil, for uptake by plant roots, or by **foliar feeding** *[applying liquid fertilizer to plant leaves]*, for uptake through leaves. Fertilizers can be organic (composed of organic matter), or inorganic (made of simple, inorganic chemicals or minerals). They can be naturally occurring compounds such as peat or mineral deposits, or manufactured through natural processes (such as composting) or chemical processes (such as the Haber process). These chemical compounds can improve the health and appearance of plants in **lawns** *[garden]* and gardens as they provide different essential nutrients that typically encourage plant growth.

They typically provide, in varying proportions, the three major plant nutrients (nitrogen, phosphorus, potassium: N-P-K), the secondary plant nutrients (calcium, sulfur, magnesium) and sometimes trace elements (or micronutrients) with a role in plant or animal nutrition: boron, chlorine, manganese, iron, zinc, copper, molybdenum and (in some countries) selenium.

Both organic and inorganic fertilizers were called "manure" derived from the French expression for manual **tillage** *[farming]*, but this term is now mostly restricted to organic manure.

It is believed by some that organic agricultural methods are more environmentally friendly and better maintain soil organic matter levels. There are generally accepted scientific studies that support this supposition. Regardless of the source, fertilization results in increased unharvested plant **biomass** *[plant materials used as fuel]* left on the soil surface and crop **residues** *[leftover part]* remaining in the soil. Too much of a vital nutrient can be as detrimental as not enough. "Fertilizer burn" can occur when too much fertilizer is applied, resulting in a drying out of the roots and damage or even death of the plant. Organic fertilizers are just as likely to burn as inorganic fertilizers. If excess nitrogen is present the plants will begin to **exude** *[issue, show]* nitrogen from the leafy areas. This is called **guttation** *[The water exuded from leaves]*.

Macronutrients and micronutrients

Fertilizers can be divided into macronutrients or micronutrients based on their concentrations in plant dry matter. There are six macronutrients: nitrogen, phosphorus, and potassium, often termed "primary macronutrients" because their availability is usually managed with NPK fertilizers, and the "secondary macronutrients"—calcium, magnesium, and sulfur—which are required in roughly similar quantities but whose availability is often managed as part of liming and manuring practices rather than fertilizers. The macronutrients are consumed in larger quantities and normally present as a whole number or tenths of percentages in plant tissues (on a dry matter weight basis). There are many micronutrients, required in concentrations ranging from 5 to 100 parts per million (ppm) by mass. Plant micronutrients include iron (Fe), manganese (Mn), boron (B), copper (Cu), molybdenum (Mo), nickel (Ni), chlorine (Cl), and zinc (Zn).

Macronutrient fertilizers

Synthesized materials are also called **artificial** *[unnatural]*, and may be described as **straight** *[invariable, direct]*, where the product predominantly contains the three primary ingredients of nitrogen (N), phosphorus (P), and potassium (K), which are known as N-P-K fertilizers or **compound fertilizers** *[mixed plant food]*when elements are mixed intentionally. They are named or labeled according to the content of these three elements, which are macronutrients.

Nitrogen fertilizer

Nitrogen fertilizer is often synthesized to produces ammonia. This ammonia is applied directly to the soil or used to produce other compounds, notably ammonium nitrate and urea, both dry, concentrated products that may be used as fertilizer materials or mixed with water to form a concentrated liquid nitrogen fertilizer, UAN. Ammonia can also be used in combination with rock phosphate and potassium fertilizer to produce compound fertilizers such as 10-10-10 or 15-15-15.

Organic and inorganic fertilizers

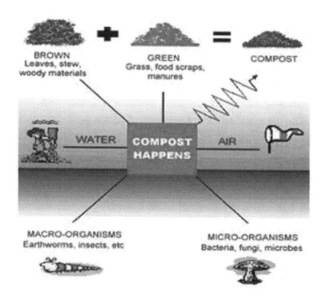

Naturally occurring organic fertilizers include manure, **slurry** *[the mixture of manure and water]*, **worm castings** *[worm manure]*, **peat** *[worm manure]*, seaweed *[kelp]*, sewage *[waste]*, and **guano** *[dung from a sea bird]*. Green manure crops are also grown to add nutrients to the soil. Naturally occurring minerals such as sulfate of potash and limestone are also considered Organic Fertilizers.

Manufactured organic fertilizers include **compost** *[mixture of various decaying organic substances]*, blood meal *[dried, powdered* *blood]*, **bone meal** *[crushed bones]* and seaweed extracts. Other examples are natural enzyme digested proteins, **fish meal** *[ground dried fish]*, and **feather meal** *[dried waste from the poultry industry]*.

Naturally occurring inorganic fertilizers (mineral fertilizers) include Chilean sodium nitrate, mined rock phosphate, and limestone (a calcium source).

a) Comprehension questions

1- What are fertilizers for?
2- How can the organic and inorganic fertilizers be produced?
3- How can chemical compounds be useful for plants?
4- What are the most important plant nutrients?
5- What does NPK mean on fertilizer bags?
6- What is the function of secondary macronutrients?
7- What is the normal share of macronutrients in plant tissue?
8- What is the other name for inorganic fertilizers? Can you name them?
9- What does 10-10-10 or 15-15-15 refer to?

b) Fill in the blanks with proper words.

Fertilizer—growth—tillage—residue—biomass— artificial—compost.

1. _____are chemical compounds given to plants to promote growth; they are usually applied either through the soil, for uptake by plant roots, or by foliar feeding, for uptake through leaves.
2. A mixture of decaying vegetation and manure; used as a fertilizer is called_____.
3. _____is the activity of preparing land for growing crops.
4. _____refers to living and recently dead biological material that can be used as fuel or for industrial production.
5. _____can be defined as an increase in size, number, value, or strength.
6. Matter that is left after something has been removed is_____.

7. A/an_____thing is something that is not natural.

c) Projects

Based on your technical knowledge, write a paragraph about one of these questions.

1- What is compost and how is it produced?
2- What are the disadvantages of over use of chemical fertilizers?
3- What are the impacts of each one of main fertilizers (Nitrogen, phosphorus, potassium) on plant growth?

d) Good to know!

Choosing Between Chemical and Organic Fertilizers

Fertilizers provide one or more of the chemical elements necessary for plant growth and development. Organic fertilizers such as manures, compost or bone meal are derived directly from plant or animal sources. Inorganic fertilizers such as ammonium sulphate or ammonium phosphate are often called commercial or synthetic fertilizers, because they go through some manufacturing process, although many of them come from naturally occurring mineral deposits. Neither type is better in every situation, because there are advantages and disadvantages to using either one. Inorganic fertilizers usually contain only a few nutrients. These nutrients are in a concentrated form readily available to plants. However, since they are lost from the soil quickly, you may have to apply it several times during the growing season unless you use a specially formulated, slow-release type.

Test your fertilizer knowledge

1 WHAT ARE THE TOP THREE
FERTILIZER-UTILIZING U.S. CROPS?

Corn, wheat and soybeans.

2 HOW MUCH FERTILIZER DOES IT TAKE
TO PRODUCE A BUSHEL OF CORN?

Depending on the type of cropping system used,
typically 1.5 to 2 pounds of fertilizer nutrients.

3 HOW MUCH FERTILIZER DOES IT TAKE
TO PRODUCE A BUSHEL OF WHEAT?

Depending on the type of cropping system used,
typically 2.5 to 3.5 pounds of fertilizer nutrients.

4 HOW MUCH FERTILIZER DOES IT TAKE
TO PRODUCE A BUSHEL OF SOYBEANS?

Depending on the type of cropping system used,
typically 1.0 to 1.5 pounds of fertilizer nutrients.

5 WHY IS FERTILIZER IMPORTANT
TO AGRICULTURE PRODUCTION?

Humans, animals and plants rely on a safe, healthy supply
of food and nutrients like nitrogen (N), phosphorus (P) and
potassium (K) for proper growth and development. Fertilizer
is the 'food' that plants – from corn and wheat to pumpkins
and apples – need to produce a healthy and bountiful crop.
All crops require nutrients in one form or another.

Chapter seven
Irrigation

Irrigation is an artificial application of water to the soil usually for assisting in growing crops. In crop production it is mainly used in dry areas and in periods of rainfall **shortfalls** *[shortage of something needed]*, but also to protect plants against **frost** *[the act or process of freezing]*. Additionally irrigation helps to suppress **weed** *[valueless plant]* growing in rice fields. In contrast, agriculture that relies only on direct rainfall is referred to as rain-fed farming. Irrigation is often studied together with **drainage** *[drain water]*, which is the natural or artificial removal of surface and sub-surface water from a given area.

Types of irrigation

Various types of irrigation techniques differ in how the water obtained from the source is distributed within the field. In general, the goal is to supply the entire field uniformly with water, so that each plant has the amount of water it needs, neither too much nor too little.

Surface irrigation

In surface irrigation systems water moves over and across the land by simple **gravity** *[heaviness or weight]* flow in order to wet it and to **infiltrate** *[to pass in by filtering]* into the soil. Surface irrigation can be subdivided into furrow, borderstrip or basin irrigation. It is often called **flood irrigation** *[the act of running water over the top of the land]* when the irrigation results in flooding or near flooding of the cultivated land *[developed land for growing]*. Historically, this has been the most common method of irrigating agricultural land.

Where water levels from the irrigation source permit, the levels are controlled by **dikes *[embankment]***, usually plugged by soil. This is often seen in terraced rice fields (rice paddies), where the method is used to flood or control the level of water in each distinct field. In some cases, the water is pumped, or lifted by human or animal power to the level of the land.

Localized irrigation

Localized irrigation is a system where water is distributed under low pressure through a piped network, in a pre-determined pattern, and applied as a small discharge to each plant or adjacent to it. **Drip *[sprinkle]*** irrigation, spray or micro-sprinkler irrigation and bubbler irrigation belong to this category of irrigation methods.

Drip Irrigation

Drip irrigation, also known as trickle irrigation, functions as its name suggests. Water is delivered at or near the root zone of plants, drop by drop. This method can be the most water-efficient method of irrigation, if managed properly, since **evaporation *[drying up]*** and **runoff *[something that drains or flows off]*** are minimized. In modern agriculture, drip irrigation is often combined with plastic mulch, further reducing evaporation, and is also the means of delivery of fertilizer. The process is known as *fertigation*.

Sprinkler irrigation

Sprinkler irrigation of blueberries in Plainville, New York

In sprinkler or overhead irrigation, water is piped to one or more central locations within the field and distributed by overhead high-pressure sprinklers or guns. A system utilizing sprinklers, sprays, or guns mounted overhead on permanently installed risers is often referred to as a *solid-set* irrigation system. Higher pressure sprinklers that **rotate** *[go around in circle]* are called *rotors* and are driven by a ball drive, gear drive, or impact mechanism. Rotors can be designed to rotate in a full or partial circle. Guns are similar to rotors, except that they generally operate at very high pressures of 40 to 130 lbf/in^2 (275 to 900 kPa) and flows of 50 to 1200 US gal/min (3 to 76 L/s), usually with nozzle diameters in the range of 0.5 to 1.9 inches (10 to 50 mm). Guns are used not only for irrigation, but also for industrial applications such as dust suppression and **logging** *[cutting down trees]*.

Sprinklers may also be mounted on moving platforms connected to the water source by a **hose** *[a flexible tube for conveying water]*. Automatically moving wheeled systems known as *traveling sprinklers* may irrigate areas such as small farms, sports fields, parks, pastures, and cemeteries unattended. Most of these utilize a length of polyethylene tubing wound on a steel drum. As the tubing is wound on the drum powered by the irrigation water or a small gas engine, the sprinkler is pulled across the field. When the sprinkler arrives back at the reel the system shuts off. This type of system is known to most people as a "water reel" traveling irrigation sprinkler and they are used extensively for dust suppression, irrigation, and land application of **waste water** *[water that* *has been used in industry]*. Other travelers use a flat rubber hose that is dragged along behind while the sprinkler platform is pulled by a cable. These cable-type travelers are definitely old technology and their use is limited in today's modern irrigation projects.

a) Comprehension Questions

1. Where is irrigation usually used?
2. Explain rain-fed farming?
3. Name different types of irrigation.
4. What are the characteristics of surface irrigation?
5. What is dike and what is it usually made of?
6. What category of irrigation methods do drip irrigation, spray or micro-sprinkler irrigation and bubbler irrigation belong to?
7. What method can be the most water-efficient method of irrigation and why is it so?
8. What are rotors?
9. What are the other uses of guns instead of irrigation?
10. How does sprinkler irrigation work?
11. What is water reel traveling irrigation sprinkler?

b) Fill in the blanks with proper words.

Irrigation, frost, dike, evaporation, waste water, hose, frost, drip irrigation

1. The slow, accurate application of water to plant root areas with a system of pipes and emitters usually operated under reduced pressure is called _____.
2. The process of a liquid converting to the gaseous is _____.
3. _____ is a wall built to prevent the sea or a river from flooding an area, or a channel dug to take water away from an area.
4. _____ is a hollow tube designed to carry fluids from one location to another.
5. An air temperature below the freezing point of water is called_____.

6. _____ is the water that has been used by some human domestic or industrial activity and, because of that, now contains waste products.

7. _____ is the controlled application of water for agricultural purposes through man-made systems to supply water requirements not satisfied by rainfall.

c) Which type of irrigation do these pictures belong to? (surface, drip, or sprinkler irrigation)

d) Good to know!

Sources of irrigation water

Sources of irrigation water can be groundwater extracted from springs or by using wells, surface water withdrawn from rivers, lakes or reservoirs or non-conventional sources like treated wastewater, desalinated water or drainage water. A special form of irrigation using surface water is spate irrigation, also called floodwater harvesting. In case of a flood (spate) water is diverted to normally dry river beds using a network of dams, gates and channels and spread over large areas. The moisture stored in the soil will be used thereafter to grow crops. Spate irrigation areas are in particular located in semi-arid or arid, mountainous regions. While floodwater harvesting belongs to the accepted irrigation methods, rainwater harvesting is usually not considered as a form of irrigation. Rainwater harvesting is the collection of runoff water from roofs or unused land and the concentration of this water on cultivated land. Therefore this method is considered as a water concentration method.

f) Project

Write a paragraph about different types of irrigation.

f) Extra reading

Sub-irrigation

Sub-irrigation also sometimes called seepage irrigation has been used for many years in field crops in areas with high water tables. It is a method of artificially raising the water table to allow the soil to be moistened from below the plants' root zone. Often those systems are located on permanent grasslands in lowlands or river valleys and combined with drainage infrastructure. A system of pumping stations, canals, weirs and gates allows it to increase or decrease the water level in a network of ditches and thereby control the water table.

Sub-irrigation is also used in commercial greenhouse production, usually for potted plants. Water is delivered from below, absorbed upwards, and the excess collected for recycling. Typically, a solution of water and nutrients floods a container or flows through a trough for a short period of time, 10-20 minutes, and is then pumped back into a holding tank for reuse. Sub-irrigation in greenhouses requires fairly sophisticated, expensive equipment and management. Advantages are water and nutrient conservation, and labor-saving through lowered system maintenance and automation. It is similar in principle and action to subsurface drip irrigation.

Chapter eight
Meteorology

Meteorology is the scientific study of the atmosphere that focuses on weather processes and **forecasting** *[weather prediction]*. Studies in the field go back **millennia** *[1000 years]*, though significant progress in meteorology did not occur until the eighteenth century. The nineteenth century saw **breakthroughs** *[important discovery]* occur after observing networks developed across several countries. Breakthroughs in weather forecasting were achieved in the second half of the twentieth century, after the development of the computer.

Meteorological phenomena are observable weather events which **illuminate** *[clarify]* and are explained by the science of meteorology. Those events are bound by the variables that exist in Earth's atmosphere. They are temperature, air pressure, water vapor, and the **gradients** *[measure of change]* and interactions of each variable, and how they change in time. The majority of Earth's observed weather is located in the troposphere. Different scales are studied to determine how systems on local, region, and global levels impact weather and climatology. Meteorology, climatology, atmospheric physics, and atmospheric chemistry are sub-disciplines of the atmospheric sciences. Meteorology and hydrology compose the interdisciplinary field of hydrometeorology. Interactions between Earth's atmosphere and the oceans are part of coupled ocean-atmosphere studies.

Equipment

Each science has its own unique sets of laboratory **equipment _[tool]_**. In the atmosphere, there are many things or qualities of the atmosphere that can be measured. Rain, which can be observed or seen anywhere and anytime, was one of the first ones to be measured historically. Also, two other accurately measured _qualities_ are **wind _[moving air]_** and **humidity _[atmospheric moisture]_**. Neither of these can be _seen_ but can be felt. The devices to measure these three appeared in the mid-15th century and were respectively the **rain gauge _[instrument that measures the amount of liquid]_**, the **anemometer _[instrument measuring wind force]_**, and the **hygrometer _[humidity instrument]_**.

The measurements taken at a weather station can include any number of atmospheric observables. Usually, temperature, pressure, wind measurements, and humidity are the variables that are measured by a thermometer, barometer, anemometer, and hygrometer, respectively. Upper air data are of crucial importance for weather forecasting. The most widely used technique is launches of radiosondes. Supplementing the radiosondes is organized by the World Meteorological Organization.

Remote sensing, as used in meteorology, is the concept of collecting data from **remote _[operated from distance]_** weather events and therefore, producing weather information. The common types of remote sensing are Radar, Lidar, and satellites. Each collects data about the atmosphere from a remote location and, usually, stores the data where the instrument is located.

Applications

Weather forecasting

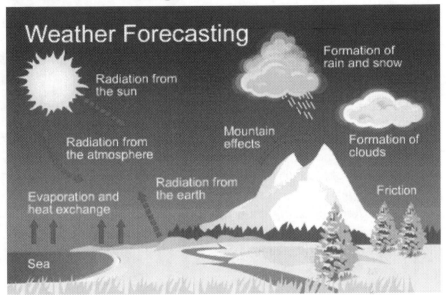

Weather forecasting is the application of science and technology to predict the state of the atmosphere for a future time and a given location. Human beings have attempted to predict the weather informally for millennia, and formally since at least the nineteenth century. Weather forecasts are made by collecting quantitative data about the current state of the atmosphere and using scientific understanding of atmospheric processes to project how the atmosphere will evolve. There are a variety of end users to weather forecasts. Weather warnings are important forecasts because they are used to protect life and property. For example, Forecasts based on temperature and precipitation are important to agriculture, and therefore to commodity traders within stock markets.

Agricultural meteorology

Meteorologists, soil scientists, agricultural **hydrologists** *[a person who studies earth's water]*, and **agronomists** *[scientist that studies soils and* *plants]* are persons concerned with studying the effects of weather and climate on plant distribution, crop yield, water-use efficiency, phonology of plant and animal development, and the energy balance of managed and natural ecosystems. They are interested in the role of vegetation on climate and weather.

Hydrometeorology

Hydrometeorology is the branch of meteorology that deals with the hydrologic cycle, the water budget, and the rainfall statistics of storms. A hydrometeorologist prepares and issues forecasts of quantitative precipitation, heavy rain, heavy snow, and highlights areas with the potential for **flash flooding** *[rapid flooding of geomorphic low-lying areas].* Typically the range of knowledge that is required overlaps with climatology and other geosciences.

Climatology

Climatology is the study of climate, scientifically defined as weather conditions **averaged** *[have something as average]* over a period of time and is a branch of the atmospheric sciences.

Differences with meteorology

In contrast to meteorology, which focuses on short term weather systems lasting up to a few weeks, climatology studies the frequency and trends of those systems. It studies the periodicity of weather events over years to millennia, as well as changes in long-term average weather patterns, in relation to atmospheric conditions. Climatologists, those who practice climatology, study both the nature of climates—local, regional or global—and the natural or human-induced factors that cause climates to change. Climatology considers the past and can help predict future climate change.

Phenomena of climatological interest include the atmospheric boundary layer, circulation patterns, heat transfer, interactions between the atmosphere and the oceans and land surface (particularly vegetation, land use and topography), and the chemical and physical composition of the atmosphere.

Climate models

Climate models use quantitative methods to **simulate** *[reproduce features of something]* the interactions of the atmosphere, oceans, land surface, and ice. They are used for a variety of purposes from study of the **dynamics** *[study of motion]* of the weather and climate system to **projections** *[estimate]* of future climate. All climate models balance, or very nearly balance, incoming energy as short wave electromagnetic radiation to the earth with outgoing energy as long wave (infrared) electromagnetic radiation from the earth. Any unbalance results in a change in the average temperature of the earth.

The most talked-about models of recent years have been those relating temperature to **emissions** *[released energy]* of carbon dioxide. These models predict an upward **trend** *[tendency]* in the surface temperature record, as well as a more rapid increase in temperature at higher altitudes.

a) Comprehension Questions

1. Define Meteorology.
2. What are Meteorological phenomena?
3. Name the variables that exist in Earth's atmosphere.
4. What qualities of atmosphere can be measured with special equipments?
5. What atmospheric qualities can be felt but can't be seen?
6. What are rain gauge, anemometer, and hygrometer used for?

7. Explain remote sensing.
8. What is the application to predict the state of the atmosphere for a future time and a given location?
9. Why are weather warnings important?
10. How are weather forecasts made?
11. Who are the persons that concerned with studying the effects of weather and climate on plant distribution?
12. What branch of meteorology does deal with the hydrologic cycle, the water budget, and the rainfall statistics of storms?
13. What is climatology?
14. What is the difference between climatology and meteorology?
15. What are climate models and what are their usages?

b) **Fill in the blanks with proper words.**

Gradient, emissions, simulate, equipment, launching, humidity, flash flooding, breakthrough, forecasting, dynamics, illuminate, trend.

1. _____ is a statement made about the future.
2. Discharge of a material or energy to the atmosphere is called _____.
3. _____ means a general direction in which something tends to move.
4. _____ is a branch of mechanics concerned with the forces that cause motions of bodies.
5. _____ is the imitation of some real thing, state of affairs, or process.
6. A _____ is a rapid flooding of geomorphic low-lying areas—washes, rivers and streams and it is caused by heavy rain.
7. The act of beginning something new is called_____.
8. _____ is a tool needed for an undertaking or to perform a service.
9. _____ refers to making an important discovery.
10. When you _____ something you make it free from confusion or ambiguity.
11. A graded measurement in the magnitude of some physical quantity or dimension is called _____.

12. _____ is the amount of water vapor in the air.

c) Pose 3 questions from the text and ask other classmates.

Global warming

Global warming is the increase in the average temperature of the Earth's near-surface air and the oceans since the mid-twentieth century and its projected continuation. Global surface temperature increased 0.74 ± 0.18 °C during the 100 years ending in 2005. Some studies show that anthropogenic greenhouse gases are responsible for most of the observed temperature increase since the middle of the twentieth century and natural phenomena such as solar variation and volcanoes probably had a small warming effect from pre-industrial times to 1950 and a small cooling effect from 1950 onward. Increasing global temperature will cause sea levels to rise and will change the amount and pattern of precipitation, likely including an expanse of the subtropical desert regions. Other likely effects include Arctic shrinkage and resulting Arctic methane release, shrinkage of the Amazon rainforest (already very damaged by deforestation from logging and farming), increases in the intensity of extreme weather events, changes in agricultural yields, modifications of trade routes, glacier retreat, species extinctions and changes in the ranges of disease vectors.

---

d) Visit this website and provide a 2 minutes speech on green house effect.

http://www.weatherquestions.com/What_is_the_greenhouse_effect.htm

e) Good to know

Expected environmental effects of global warming

Although it is difficult to connect specific weather events to global warming, an increase in global temperatures may in turn cause broader changes, including glacial retreat, Arctic shrinkage, and worldwide sea level rise. Changes in the amount and pattern of precipitation may result in flooding and drought. There may also be changes in the frequency and intensity of extreme weather events. These changes are not likely to be reversible on timescales shorter than a thousand years. Other effects may include changes in agricultural yields, addition of new trade routes, reduced summer streamflows, species extinctions, and increases in the range of disease vectors.

Additional anticipated effects include sea level rise of 0.18 to 0.59 meters (0.59 to 1.9 ft) in 2090-2100 relative to 1980-1999, repercussions to agriculture, possible slowing of the thermohaline circulation, reductions in the ozone layer, increasingly intense (but less frequent) hurricanes and extreme weather events, lowering of ocean pH, oxygen depletion in the oceans, and the spread of diseases such as malaria.

f) Project: Write a paragraph on one of these issues and then present it in class.

1. Carbon Dioxide and global warming
2. Meteorology equipments
3. Global warming
4. Greenhouse effect

g) Extra Reading

Related climatic issues of global warming

A variety of issues are often raised in relation to global warming. One is ocean acidification. Increased atmospheric CO_2 increases the amount of CO_2 dissolved in the oceans. CO_2 dissolved in the ocean reacts with water to form carbonic acid, resulting in acidification. Ocean surface pH is estimated to have decreased from 8.25 near the beginning of the industrial era to 8.14 by 2004, and is projected to decrease by a further 0.14 to 0.5 units by 2100 as the ocean absorbs more CO_2. Since organisms and ecosystems are adapted to a narrow range of pH, this raises extinction concerns, directly driven by increased atmospheric CO_2, that could prevent food webs and impact human societies that depend on marine ecosystem services.

Global dimming, the gradual reduction in the amount of global direct irradiance at the Earth's surface, may have partially mitigated global warming in the late 20th century. From 1960 to 1990 human-caused aerosols likely precipitated this effect. Scientists have stated with 66–90% confidence that the effects of human-caused aerosols, along with volcanic activity, have offset some of the global warming, and that greenhouse gases would have resulted in more warming than observed if not for these dimming agents.

Ozone depletion, the steady decline in the total amount of ozone in Earth's stratosphere, is frequently cited in relation to global warming. Although there are areas of linkage, the relationship between the two is not strong.

Chapter nine
Agriculture Machinery

Agricultural machinery is one of the most revolutionary and impactful applications of modern technology. The truly **elemental** *[basic]* human need for food has often driven the development of technology and machines. Over the last 250 years, advances in farm equipment have transformed the way people are employed and produce their food worldwide.

The first person to turn from the hunting and gathering lifestyle to farming probably did so by using his bare hands, and perhaps some sticks or stones. Tools such as knives, scythes, and wooden **plough** *[dig up ground for cultivation]* (in US: plow) were eventually developed, and dominated agriculture for thousands of years. During this time, almost everyone worked in agriculture, because each family could barely raise enough food for themselves with the limited technology of the day.

With the coming of the Industrial Revolution and the development of more complicated machines, farming methods took a great leap forward. Instead of **harvesting** *[gathering of crops]* grain by hand with a sharp blade, wheeled machines cut a continuous **swath** *[dried grass]*. Instead of threshing the grain by beating it with sticks, threshing machines separated the seeds from the heads and stalks.

These machines required a lot of power, which was originally supplied by horses or other domesticated animals. With the invention of steam power came the portable engine and later the traction engine.

Gasoline, and later diesel engines, became the main source of power for the next generation of tractors. These engines also contributed to the development of the self-propelled, combined harvester and **thresher** *[a*

78

harvester of a crop with a machine], or combine for short. Instead of cutting the grain stalks and transporting them to a stationary threshing machine, these combines cut, threshed, and separated the grain while moving continuously through the field.

Types

Combines might have taken the harvesting job away from tractors, but tractors still do the majority of work on a modern farm. They are used to pull implements—machines that till the ground, plant seed, or perform a number of other tasks.

Tillage implements prepare the soil for planting by loosening the soil and killing weeds or competing plants. The best-known is the plough, the ancient implement that was upgraded in 1838 by a man named John Deere. Ploughs are actually used less frequently in the U.S. today, with offset disks used instead to turn over the soil and chisels used to gain the depth needed to retain moisture.

The most common type of seeder is called a planter and spaces seeds out equally in long rows, which are usually 2 to 3 feet (60 to 90 cm) apart. Some crops are planted by drills, which put out much more seed in rows less than a foot apart, **blanketing *[covering layer]*** the field with crops.

After planting, other implements can be used to cultivate weeds from between rows, or to spread fertilizer and pesticides. Hay balers can be used to tightly package grass or alfalfa into a storable form for the winter months.

Tractor

A tractor is a vehicle specifically designed to deliver a high tractive effort at slow speeds. The farm tractor is used for pulling or pushing agricultural machinery or **trailer** *[towed vehivle]*, for ploughing, tilling, disking, **harrowing** *[break up land]*, planting, and similar tasks. Most commonly, the term is used to describe the distinctive farm vehicle: agricultural implements may be towed behind or mounted on the tractor, and the tractor may also provide a source of power if the implement is mechanized.

Plough

The plough is a tool used in farming for initial cultivation of soil in preparation for sowing seed or planting. It has been a basic instrument for most of recorded history, and represents one of the major advances in agriculture. The primary purpose of ploughing is to turn over the upper layer of the soil, bringing fresh nutrients to the surface, while burying weeds and the remains of previous crops, allowing them to break down. It also aerates the soil, and allows it to hold moisture better. In modern use, a ploughed field is typically left to dry out, and is then harrowed before planting.

Ploughs were initially pulled by **oxen** *[cows or bulls]*, and later in many areas by horses. In industrialized countries, the first mechanical means of pulling a plough used steam-power (ploughing engines or steam tractors), but these were gradually superseded by today's tractors. In the past two decades plough use has reduced in some areas (where soil damage and erosion are problems), in favor of shallower ploughing and other less invasive tillage techniques.

Mould board plough

A major advance in plough design was the mould board plough (American spelling: mold board plow), which aided the cutting blade. The **coulter** *[sharp blade or wheel attached to the beam of a plow]*, *knife* or skeith cuts **vertically** *[at right angle to horizon]* into the ground just ahead of the **share** *[same as ploughshare]* a wedge-shaped surface to the front and bottom of the mould board with the landside of the frame supporting the below-ground components. The upper parts of the frame carry (from the front) the coupling for the motive power (horses), the coulter and the landside frame. Depending on the size of the implement, and the number of furrows it is designed to plough at one time, there is a wheel or wheels positioned to support the frame.

When **dragged** *[pull something along with effort]* through a field the coulter cuts down into the soil and the share cuts horizontally from the previous furrow to the vertical cut. This releases a **rectangular strip** *[a band shape like rectangle]* of **sod** *[ground or soil]* that is then lifted by the share and carried by the mould board up and over, so that the strip of sod that is being cut lifts and rolls over as the plough moves forward, dropping back to the ground upside down into the furrow and onto the turned soil from the previous run down the field. Each gap in the ground where the soil has been lifted and moved across (usually to the right) is called a **furrow** *[trench in ploughed field]*.

Disc harrow

A disc harrow is a farm implement that is used to cultivate the soil where crops are to be planted. It is also used to **chop** *[cut something up with sharp tool]* up unwanted weeds or crop remainders. It consists of many iron or steel discs which have slight concavity and are arranged into two or four sections. When viewed from above, the four sections would appear to form an "X" which has been flattened to be wider than it is tall. The discs are also offset so that they are not parallel with the overall direction of the implement. This is so they slice the ground they cut over a little bit to optimize the result. The concavity of the discs as well as their being offset causes them to loosen and pickup the soil they cut.

Rotary tiller

A rotary tiller, also known as a rototiller, rotavator, rotary hoe, power tiller, or rotary plough is a motorized cultivator that works the soil by means of rotating **tines** *[a sharp, projecting point]* or blades. Rotary tillers are either self propelled or drawn as an attachment behind either a two-wheel tractor or four-wheel tractor. For two-wheel tractors they are rigidly fixed and powered via couplings to the tractors' transmission. For four-wheel tractors they are attached by means of a three-point hitch and driven by a Power Take-Off (PTO).

Seed drill

A sowing machine which uses the seed drill concept

A seed drill is a device for planting seeds in the soil. Before the introduction of the seed drill, the common practice was to "**broadcast**" *[scatter seeds]* seeds by hand. Besides being wasteful, broadcasting was very imprecise and led to a poor distribution of seeds, leading to low productivity.

The seed drill allows farmers to sow seeds in well-spaced rows at specific depths at a specific seed rate; each tube creates a hole of a specific depth, drops in a seed, and covers it over. Prior to this, farmers simply cast seeds on the ground, by hand, for them to grow where they landed (broadcasting).

Combine harvester

The combine harvester, or simply combine, is a machine that harvests grain crops. The objective is to complete three processes, which used to be distinct, in one pass of the machine over a particular part of the field. Among the crops harvested with a combine are wheat, oats, rye, barley, corn (maize), soybeans, and flax (linseed). The waste straw left behind on the field is the remaining dried **stems** *[main axis of plant]* and leaves of the crop with limited nutrients which is either chopped and spread on the field or baled for feed and **bedding** *[bed for animals]* for livestock.

a) Comprehension Questions

1. What were the first tools of harvesting?
2. What happened during industrial revolution?
3. What was the pitfall of wheeled machines?
4. Name the last generation of agriculture machinery.
5. What are different types of harvesting machines?
6. What do the tillage implements do to the soil?
7. Name a seeder and explain how it works.
8. How is a tractor working?
9. What is plough and describe how it works?
10. Explain the systematic working of a mould board plough.
11. What are the applications of disc harrow?
12. Name a motorized cultivator and explain its usage.
13. What are the features of rotary tillers and what are their functions?
14. Name a machine that plant seeds in the soil and describe how they make the farmers work easier.
15. How does a combine harvester work?

b) Fill in the blanks with proper words.

Broadcast, plough, furrow, thresher, stem, sod, elemental, harvest, oxen, harrows.

1. _____ are commonly adult, male cattle, but cows (adult females) or bulls (fertile males) may also be used in some areas.
2. Surface layer of ground containing a mat of grass and grass roots is called _____.
3. _____ is a narrow trench in soil made by a plough.
4. _____ means to sow seeds by scattering them by hand.
5. In agriculture, a set of _____ is an implement for cultivating the surface of the soil.
6. _____ is a farm tool having one or more heavy blades to break the soil and cut a furrow prior to sowing.
7. _____ is a slender structure that supports a plant or fungus or a plant part or plant organ.
8. The crop that is gathered or ripens during a season is called _____.
9. _____ means basic and essentials.
10. _____ is a farm machine for separating seeds or grain from the husks and straw.

c) Good to know!

Chisel plough

The chisel plough is a common tool to get deep tillage (prepared land) with limited soil disruption. The main function of this plough is to loosen and aerate the soils while leaving crop residue at the top of the soil. This plough can be used to reduce the effects of compaction and to help break up plough pan and hardpan. Unlike many other ploughs the chisel will not invert or turn the soil. This characteristic has made it a useful addition to no-till and limited-tillage farming practices which attempt to maximize the erosion-prevention benefits of keeping organic matter and farming residues present on the soil surface through the year. Because of these attributes, the use of a chisel plough is considered by some to be more sustainable than other types of plough, such as the mould-board plough.

d) Visit this website and get some information about these machines, then match the pictures with the right machine.

http://www.history.rochester.edu/Appleton/a/agmac-m.html

a) Stump Pullers

b) Cold Crushers

c) Fanning Mills

d) Potato Digger

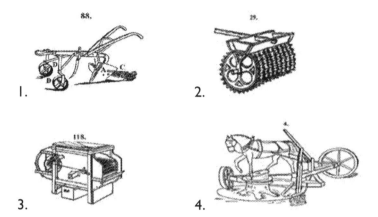

1.

2.

3.

4.

e) **Check this website, then choose I machine from it and tell your classmates about in the form of a small lecture.**

http://agricoop.nic.in/dacdivision/machinery1/contents.htm

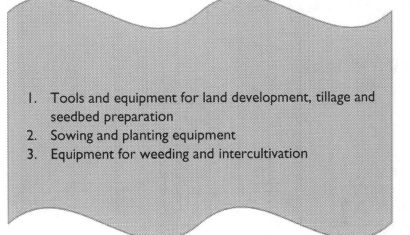

1. Tools and equipment for land development, tillage and seedbed preparation
2. Sowing and planting equipment
3. Equipment for weeding and intercultivation

Chapter ten
Plant pathology

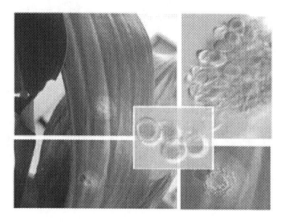

Plant pathology (also phytopathology) is the scientific study of plant diseases caused by pathogens (**infectious** *[caused by bacteria]* diseases) and environmental conditions (physiological factors). Organisms that cause infectious disease include fungi, oomycetes, bacteria, viruses, viroids, virus-like organisms, phytoplasmas, protozoa, nematodes and parasitic plants. Plant pathology also involves the study of pathogen identification, disease **etiology** *[cause of disease]*, disease cycles, economic impact, plant disease epidemiology, plant disease resistance, how plant diseases affect humans and animals, pathosystem genetics, and management of plant diseases.

The *"Disease triangle"* is a central concept of plant pathology. It is based on the principle that infectious diseases develop, or do not develop, based on three-way interactions between the host, the pathogen, and environmental conditions.

Plant pathogens

Fungi

The majority of phytopathogenic fungi belong to the Ascomycetes and the Basidiomycetes.

The fungi reproduce both sexually and asexually via the production of **spores** *[asexual reproductive structure]*. These spores may be spread long distances by air or water, or they may be soil borne. Many soil—borne spores, normally **zoospores** *[spore capable of independent motion]* and capable of living **saprotrophically** *[feeding on dead matter]*, carrying out the first part of their lifecycle in the soil.

Fungal diseases can be controlled through the use of fungicides in agriculture, however new races of fungi often **evolve** *[develop gradually]* that are resistant to various fungicides.

Oomycetes

The oomycetes are not true fungi but are fungal-like organisms. They include some of the most destructive plant pathogens including the genus *Phytophthora* which includes the causal agents of potato late blight and sudden oak death.

Despite not being closely related to the fungi, the oomycetes have developed very similar infection strategies and so many plant pathologists group them with fungal pathogens.

Bacteria

Most bacteria that are associated with plants are actually saprotrophic, and do no harm to the plant itself. However, a small number, around 100 species, are able to cause disease. Bacterial diseases are much more prevalent in sub-tropical and tropical regions of the world.

Most plant pathogenic bacteria are rod shaped (bacilli). In order to be able to colonise the plant they have specific pathogenicity factors.

Viruses, viroids and virus-like organisms

There are many types of plant virus, and some are even **asymptomatic** *[without obvious symptoms]*. Normally plant viruses only cause a loss of **yield** *[amount produced]*. Therefore it is not economically viable to try to control them, the exception being when they infect **perennial** *[lasting over two years]* species, such as fruit trees.

Most plant viruses have small, single stranded RNA genomes. These genomes may only encode 3 or 4 proteins: a replicase, a coat protein, a movement protein to allow cell to cell movement though plasmodesmata and sometimes a protein that allows transmission by a **vector** *[disease-transmitting organism]*.

Plant viruses must be transmitted from plant to plant by a vector. This is often by an insect (for example aphids), but some fungi, nematodes and protozoa have been shown to be viral vectors.

Nematodes

Nematodes are small, multi-cellular wormlike creatures. Many live freely in the soil, but there are some species which **parasitize** *[infest organism as parasite]* plant roots. They are a problem in tropical and subtropical regions of the world, where they may infect crops. Potato cyst nematodes are widely distributed in Europe and North and South America and cause $300 million worth of damage in Europe every year. Root knot nematodes have quite a large host range, whereas cyst nematodes tend to only be able to infect a few species. Nematodes are able to cause radical changes in root cells in order to facilitate their lifestyle.

Protozoa

There are a few examples of plant diseases caused by protozoa. They are transmitted as zoospores which are very durable, and may be able to survive in a resting state in the soil for many years. They have also been shown to transmit plant viruses.

When the **motile** *[capable of movement]* zoospores come into contact with a root hair they produce a plasmodium and **invade** *[enter and spread through something]* the roots.

Insect biodiversity

In agricultural ecosystems, biodiversity is instrumentally important not only for the production of food, but for other ecological services as well, including the recycling of nutrients, regulation of microclimate and local hydrological processes, suppression of undesirable organisms and **detoxification** *[process of removing poison]* of **noxious** *[harmful]* chemicals.

In the United States alone, pollination by bees accounts for over US$9 billion of economic revenue. According to some estimates, over ⅓ of the human diet can be traced directly or indirectly to bee pollination. Losses of key pollinators have been reported in at least one region or country on every continent except Antarctica, which has no pollinators. The Millennium Ecosystem Assessment concluded that with the global decline in the amount of pollinators, there is not a complete loss of fruit or seeds, but a significant decrease in quantity and viability in fruits, and a lower number of seeds.

Part of these insects can cause serious damages in crops and, consequently, lead to less yielding. These insects are known as **pests** *[damaging organism]*.

Pest control

Pest control refers to the regulation or management of a species defined as a pest, usually because it is perceived to be **detrimental** *[harmful]* to a person's health, the ecology or the economy.

Pest control is at least as old as agriculture, as there has always been a need to keep crops free from pests. In order to maximize food production, it is advantageous to protect crops from competing species of plants, as well as from herbivores competing with humans.

The conventional approach was probably the first to be employed, since it is comparatively easy to destroy weeds by burning them or ploughing them under, and to kill larger competing herbivores, such as crows and other birds eating seeds. Techniques such as **crop rotation** *[growing a series of dissimilar types of crops in the same area in sequential seasons]*, companion planting (also known as intercropping or mixed cropping), and the selective breeding of pest-resistant **cultivars** *[plant variety produced by breeding]* have a long history.

Many pests have only become a problem because of the direct actions of humans. Modifying these actions can often substantially reduce the pest problem.

a) Comprehension Question

1. What is Plant Pathology?
2. Name some organisms that cause infectious disease.
3. What is the central concept of plant pathology?
4. To which category do the majority of phytopathogenic fungi belong?
5. How are the fungi reproducing?
6. How are the spores spread?
7. What are zoospores?
8. How can fungal diseases be controlled?
9. What are oomycetes and what features do they have?
10. What do plant viruses cause?
11. Why is it not economically viable to control viruses?

12. What is the role of genomes in plant viruses?
13. How the plant viruses are transmitted from plant to plant?
14. What are nematodes and where do they live?
15. In what regions are nematodes problematic?
16. How protozoa are transmitted?
17. How do motile zoospores invade the roots?
18. Why biodiversity is instrumentally important in agricultural ecosystems?
19. What are pests?
20. What are some techniques for pest control?

b) Fill in the blanks with proper words.

parasitism, spore, etiology, evolve, perennial, crop, asymptomatic, Infectious, zoospore, detoxification, crop rotation.

1. A farming practice in which the same land is used to grow different crops in successive seasons or years is called_____.
2. _____can be caused by bacteria, viruses, or other microorganisms.
3. _____is the set of factors that contributes to the occurrence of a disease.
4. A small usually single-celled asexual reproductive body produced by many nonflowering plants and fungi and some bacteria is refered to as_____.
5. _____is a spore of some algae and fungi that is capable of independent movement.
6. To develop something gradually, often into something more complex or advanced, or undergo such development means_____.
7. _____describes a plant that lasts for more than two growing seasons, either dying back after each season.
8. _____is a type of symbiotic relationship between two different organisms where one organism, takes favor from the host.
9. _____is a group of plants grown by people for food or other use, especially on a large scale in farming or horticulture.
10. The process of removing a toxic substance from something or counteracting its toxic effects is_____.

c) Good to know!

Insect

Insects are arthropods, having a hard exoskeleton, a three-part body (head, thorax, and abdomen), three pairs of jointed legs, compound eyes, and two antennae. The head holds large compound eyes, antenna (feelers), and the mouthpart. The legs (and wings, if applicable) are attached to the thorax. On most insects, the abdomen is not an outstanding feature composed of 11 segments. On grasshoppers, there is a large round disc on the first segment next to the thorax. It is called a tympanum and is the grasshopper's ear. And on each abdominal segment, there is a small breathing hole called the thoracic spiracle.

Insects are the most diverse group of animals on the planet. There are approximately 2,200 species of praying mantis, 5,000 dragonfly, 20,000 grasshopper, 82,000 true bug, 120,000 fly, 110,000 bee, wasp, ant and sawfly, 170,000 butterfly and moth, and 360,000 beetle species described to date. Estimates of the total number of current species, including those not yet known to science, range from two million to fifty million, with newer studies favoring a lower figure of about six to ten million. With over a million described species—more than half of all known living organisms—insects potentially represent over 90% of the differing life forms on the planet. They are most diverse at the equator and their diversity declines toward the poles. Insects may be found in nearly all environments on the planet, although only a small number of species occur in the oceans, a habitat dominated by another arthropod group, the crustaceans.

d) Project

1. Get some information about different ways for pest control.
2. Surf the internet and find 3 website on the issues discussed in this lesson and introduce them to the class.

e) Extra Reading

Reproduction

Most insects hatch from eggs, but some are ovoviviparous or viviparous, and all undergo a series of moults as they develop and grow in size. This manner of growth is necessitated by the inelastic exoskeleton. Moulting is a process by which the individual escapes the confines of the exoskeleton in order to increase in size, then grows a new and larger outer covering. In some insects, the young are called nymphs and are similar in form to the adult except that the wings are not developed until the adult stage. In other species, an egg hatches to produce a larva are generally worm-like in form, The larva grows and eventually becomes a pupa, a stage marked by reduced movement and often sealed within a cocoon.

In the pupal stage, the insect undergoes considerable change in form to emerge as an adult, or imago. Butterflies are an example of an insect that undergoes complete metamorphosis.

Chapter eleven
Sustainable agriculture

Sustainable development

Sustainable development is a pattern of resource use that aims to meet human needs while preserving the environment so that these needs can be met not only in the present, but also for future generations to come.

The United Nations Division for Sustainable Development lists the following areas as some of the scope of sustainable development:

- Agriculture
- Atmosphere
- Biodiversity
- Biotechnology
- Climate Change

- Consumption and Production Patterns
- Desertification and Drought
- Energy
- Systems ecology
- Forests
- Fresh Water
- Health
- International Cooperation for Enabling Environment
- Land management
- Mountains
- National Sustainable Development Strategies
- Oceans and Seas
- Sanitation
- Science
- Technology
- Toxic Chemicals
- Water

Sustainable agriculture

Sustainable agriculture refers to the ability of a farm to produce food without causing severe or irreversible damage to ecosystem health. Two key issues are biophysical (the long-term effects of various practices on soil properties and processes essential for crop productivity) and socio-economic (the long-term ability of farmers to obtain inputs and manage resources such as labor).

The physical aspects of sustainability are partly understood. Practices that can cause long-term damage to soil include excessive tillage (leading to erosion) and irrigation without adequate drainage (leading to **salinization** *[treat something with salt]*). Long-term experiments have provided some of the best data on how various practices affect soil properties essential to sustainability.

Although air and sunlight are available everywhere on Earth, crops also depend on soil nutrients and the availability of water. When farmers grow and harvest crops, they remove some of these nutrients from the soil. Without **replenishment** *[nourish]*, land suffers from nutrient **depletion** *[replacement]* and becomes either unusable or suffers from reduced yields. Sustainable agriculture depends on replenishing the soil while minimizing the use of non-renewable resources, such as natural gas (used in converting atmospheric nitrogen into synthetic fertilizer), or **mineral ores** *[minerals from which metal is extracted]* (e.g., phosphate). Possible sources of nitrogen that would be available include:

1. recycling crop waste and livestock or human manure
2. growing legume crops and **forages** *[food for animals]* such as peanuts or alfalfa that form **symbioses** *[close association of animals or plants]* with nitrogen-fixing bacteria called rhizobia
3. industrial production of nitrogen by the Haber Process uses hydrogen, which is currently derived from natural gas, (but this hydrogen could instead be made by electrolysis of water using electricity (perhaps from solar cells or windmills))
4. genetically engineering (non-legume) crops to form nitrogen-fixing symbioses or fix nitrogen without microbial symbionts.

The last option was proposed in the 1970s, but would be well beyond the capability of early 21st century technology, even if various concerns about biotechnology were addressed. Sustainable options for replacing other nutrient inputs (phosphorus, potassium, etc.) are more limited. An often overlooked option is **landraces** *[breed of hog]* that are adapted to less than ideal conditions such as drought or lack of nutrients.

In some areas, sufficient rainfall is available for crop growth, but many other areas require irrigation. For irrigation systems to be sustainable they require proper management (to avoid salinization) and mustn't use more water from their source than is naturally replenished, otherwise the water source becomes, in effect, a non-renewable resource. Improvements in water well drilling technology and the development of **submersible pumps** *[underwater pumps]* have made it possible for large crops to be regularly grown where reliance on rainfall alone previously made this level of success unpredictable. However, this progress has come at a price, in that in many areas where this has occurred, such as the Ogallala Aquifer, the water is being used at a greater rate than its rate of recharge.

Sustainable agriculture was also addressed by the 1990 farm bill.

It was defined as follows:

"the term sustainable agriculture means an **integrated** *[combined]* system of plant and animal production practices having a site-specific application that over the long term will:

- satisfy human food and fiber needs
- enhance environmental quality and the natural resource base upon which the agricultural economy depends
- make the most efficient use of nonrenewable resources and on-farm resources and integrate, where appropriate, natural biological cycles and controls
- sustain the economic **viability** *[practicable or worthwhile]* of farm operations
- enhance the quality of life for farmers and society as a whole."

Sustainable agriculture has many different branches of which "the organic farming" is the oldest and the most important sub-discipline of this notion.

Organic farming

Organic farming is a form of agriculture that relies on crop rotation, green manure, compost, biological pest control, and mechanical cultivation to maintain soil productivity and control pests excluding or limiting the use of synthetic fertilizers and synthetic pesticides, plant growth regulators, livestock feed additives, and genetically modified organisms. Since 1990, the market for organic products has grown at a rapid pace, to reach $46 billion in 2007. This demand has driven a similar increase in organically managed farmland. Approximately 32.2 million hectares worldwide are now farmed organically, representing approximately 0.8 percent of total world farmland. In addition, as of 2007 organic wild products are harvested on approximately 30 million hectares.

International Federation of Organic Agriculture Movements (IFOAM) defines the goal of organic farming as follows:

"Organic agriculture is a production system that sustains the health of soils, ecosystems and people. It relies on ecological processes, biodiversity and cycles adapted to local conditions, rather than the use of inputs with adverse effects. Organic agriculture combines tradition, innovation and science to benefit the shared environment and promote fair relationships and a good quality of life for all involved."

a) Comprehension Questions

1. What do we mean by sustainable development?
2. Name different areas of sustainable development.
3. What is sustainable agriculture?
4. What are the two key issues in sustainable agriculture?
5. What issues can cause long-term damage to soil?
6. What do crops depend on?
7. Name different possible sources of nitrogen.
8. What are the benefits and pitfalls of water well drilling technology and the development of submersible pumps?
9. Define sustainable agriculture as it was addressed by the 1990 farm bill.
10. What are different branches of sustainable agriculture?
11. What is organic farming and what does it rely on?

b) Fill in the blanks with proper words.

Integrated, symbioses, replenishment, viability, pest, forages, salinization, landrace, mineral ores, depletion, crop rotation.

1. Soil_____is the salt content in the soil.
2. _____means filling somebody or something with needed energy or nourishment.

3. To use up or reduce something such as supplies, resources, or energy is called_____.

4. _____is a naturally occurring mineral from which constituents, especially metals, can be profitably extracted.

5. _____refers to food for animals, especially crops grown to feed horses, cattle, and other livestock.

6. A close association of animals or plants of different species that is often, but not always, of mutual benefit is named_____.

7. _____is a northern European hog belonging to a white lean long-bodied breed developed in Denmark.

8. Made up of aspects or parts that work well together means_____.

9. _____means able to be done or worth doing.

10. _____is an organism that is damaging to livestock, crops, humans, or land fertility.

11. A farming practice in which the same land is used to grow different crops in successive seasons or years is called_____.

c) Good to know!

Soil management

Enhancing soil health is important for organic farmers, but providing enough nutrients, particularly nitrogen, is often a challenge for organic farmers. Plants primarily need nitrogen, phosphorus, and potassium. Crop rotation and green manure help to provide adequate nutrition. Intercropping, which is sometimes used for insect and disease control, can also increase soil nutrients. Cover cropping, application of compost, and mulching can also increase organic matter. Organic farmers can also use certain processed fertilizers such as seed meal and various mineral powders such as rock phosphate and greensand, a naturally occurring form of potash which provides potassium. Altogether these methods help to control erosion, promote biodiversity, and enhance the health of the soil. In some cases pH may need to be amended. Natural pH amendments include lime and sulfur, but in the U.S. some synthetically compounds such as iron sulfate, aluminum sulfate, magnesium sulfate, and soluble boron products are allowed in organic farming.

d) Extra reading

Why farm organically?

Organic farming provides long-term benefits to people and the environment.

Organic farming aims to:

- increase long-term soil fertility
- control pests and diseases without harming the environment
- ensure that water stays clean and safe.
- use resources which the farmer already has, so the farmer needs less money to buy farm inputs.
- produce nutritious food, feed for animals and high quality crops to sell at a good price.

Modern, intensive agriculture causes many problems, including the following:

- Artificial fertilizers and herbicides are easily washed from the soil and pollute rivers, lakes and water courses.
- The prolonged use of artificial fertilizers results in soils with a low organic matter content which is easily eroded by wind and rain.
- Dependency on fertilizers. Greater amounts are needed every year to produce the same yields of crops.
- Artificial pesticides can stay in the soil for a long time and enter the food chain where they build up in the bodies of animals and humans, causing health problems.
- Artificial chemicals destroy soil micro-organisms resulting in poor soil structure and aeration and decreasing nutrient availability.
- Pests and diseases become more difficult to control as they become resistant to artificial pesticides. The numbers of natural enemies decrease because of pesticide use and habitat loss.